ELLEN JAFFE JONES

recipes by
ALAN ROETTINGER

plant-based primal recipes

Book Publishing Company

Summertown, Tennessee

Library of Congress Cataloging-in-Publication Data

Jones, Ellen Jaffe.
  Vegan paleo / Ellen Jaffe Jones ; recipes by Alan Roettinger.
    pages cm
  Includes bibliographical references and index.
  ISBN 978-1-57067-305-4 (pbk. : alk. paper) — ISBN 978-1-57067-894-3 (e-book)
1. Vegan cooking. 2. High-protein diet—Recipes. 3. Prehistoric peoples—
Nutrition. I. Roettinger, Alan. II. Title.
  TX837.J54293 2014
  641.5'636—dc23

                                                                    2014004613

Color photos: Andrew William Schmidt
Food styling: Ron Maxen
Cover and interior design: John Wincek

Printed on recycled paper

Book Publishing Co. is a member of Green Press Initiative. We chose to print this title on paper with post-consumer recycled content, processed without chlorine, which saved the following natural resources:

40 trees
1,266 pounds of solid waste
18,920 gallons of wastewater
3,488 pounds of greenhouse gases
18 million BTUs of total energy

For more information, visit greenpressinitiative.org.

Paper calculations from Environmental Defense Paper Calculator, edf.org/papercalculator.

Printed in Canada

Book Publishing Company
P.O. Box 99
Summertown, TN 38483
888-260-8458
bookpubco.com

ISBN 13: 978-1-57067-305-4

20 19 18 17 16 15 14   1 2 3 4 5 6 7 8 9

Calculations for the nutritional analyses in this book are based on the average number of servings listed with the recipes and the average amount of an ingredient if a range is called for. Calculations are rounded up to the nearest gram. If two options for an ingredient are listed, the first one is used. The analyses include oil used for frying. Not included are optional ingredients and serving suggestions.

contents

Acknowledgments

Ellen Jaffe Jones This book is dedicated to every person who doesn't believe it's possible to win a race on a vegan diet. Deep gratitude goes to the doctors who ordered me to change my diet and lifestyle so I didn't end up sick and suffering for decades from excruciating diseases and medical complications like everyone else in my family. Dr. Gary Wasserman, thanks for being the voice of reason and going against conventional wisdom!

To my publisher, Book Publishing Company, thank you for your ongoing support. I am endlessly grateful to publishing gurus Bob and Cynthia Holzapfel for their wisdom, and to Jo Stepaniak for her sage advice and editing expertise. On book tours, Thomas Hupp, John Schweri, and Barbara and Warren Jefferson have kept me energized and laughing so hard my sides hurt.

A big thanks to Alan Roettinger for his recipe wizardry in the kitchen and whose sense of humor keeps us all sane on social media and in real life. I love his creativity and intuitive abilities to imagine and design contemporary recipes based on ancient times. It has been an honor to coauthor this book with him.

Alan Roettinger As always, I must acknowledge the power and consciousness of life, without which my existence would never have occurred, much less the recipes in this book. I am most grateful for it, not only because I am alive, but also because even the slightest awareness of it brings me inexpressible joy. Nothing is more precious or beautiful than life itself.

I'm very grateful for my wonderful wife and son, my sisters—alive and departed—and for my many friends and associates, all of whom add rich context and exquisite texture to the meaning of my life. Without them, my projects would be a dull, fruitless enterprise.

I'm also grateful for hunger; without it, food would have no meaning, the enjoyment of living would be horribly impoverished, and I'd be out of a job.

Once again, as three times before, I'm grateful for the entire clan at Book Publishing Company, who not only have cheerfully joined me in yet another adventure, but who also inspire me deeply with their seamless teamwork and their unique way of living earnestly.

Finally—once again—I'm grateful for my incomparable editor; I seem to argue less with her each time around, and this I attribute to the marvelous free education I'm receiving, courtesy of her indomitable correctness. My success as a writer is at least half her doing.

Preface

Given that animal protein is a major component of any standard paleo diet, how can anyone be a vegan and still go paleo? Well, as we all know, things aren't always what they seem. Actually, the similarities between paleo and vegan diets are pretty substantial. The only items vegans would remove from the paleo menu are the animal-based products. Most of the other foods espoused by paleo enthusiasts are in harmony with veganism and are great for your health. Vegans may also find that many qualities of the paleo lifestyle—especially the focus on fresh and natural foods, exercise, and proper rest—intuitively make sense.

In addition to being an author, a personal trainer, and an accomplished runner, I've spent most of my life exploring healthy dietary options in direct response to the chronic diseases in my family. I was the only healthy one, and doctors said to me at an early age, "Either do things differently than everyone else in your family or you're going to end up like them." Those words planted a seed in me that would lead to regular exercise and a balanced vegan diet, which I've maintained for most of the past three decades.

I was motivated to write my first book, *Eat Vegan on $4 a Day*, because I saw too many people loading shopping carts with junk food. Many such people commented to me, "You just can't eat well on a budget." I begged to differ and illustrated my point with affordable vegan recipes.

Then came my next book, *Kitchen Divided*, which was inspired by some of the responses I got when I was on tour talking about my first book. I asked my audiences, "How difficult is it for those of you in a marriage in which one partner is veg and one is not?" Turns out, this divide creates tension in many households. So I shared my best tips for making peace, deliciously, in the kitchen.

In this, my third book, I explore various paleo diets and will show you precisely why paleo and vegan can be joined in *healthy* matrimony. Just one thing: when vegan weds paleo, cheating is allowed, at least in dietary terms. Cheating, as described in popular paleo books, simply means allowing the incorporation of up to 15 to 20 percent of non-paleo foods in your diet. For someone with a typical paleo diet, that might include a morning latte or a handful of peanuts. For the vegan who's considering paleo alternatives but wants to maintain a plant-based diet, cheat foods might include beans and grains. Such compromises can make the bridge between paleo and vegan virtually effortless to cross.

Even as a thriving vegan, you can only enhance your well-being by selectively integrating some paleo principles into your lifestyle. If you're not a vegan but are concerned about having too much meat in your diet, the paleo-vegan path may help you increase your options. As you explore the possibilities presented in this book, keep in mind that the paleo-vegan net is wide enough to comfortably support your preferences. The diversity and flexibility offered here liberate you from having to make an either-or decision. With this union, I strongly believe you can find a healthy and enjoyable way to eat, especially with the amazing, delicious recipes included here from acclaimed vegan chef Alan Roettinger.

Enjoy the best of both worlds. The advantages of the paleo-vegan approach are many, and as you'll see as you delve into this book, you *can* have your vegan cake and eat paleo too!

CHAPTER ONE

Introduction

When the paleo craze first kicked in, I have to admit, it annoyed me. There I was, publicly applaud-ing well-known vegan athletes who are proving that eating vegan actually enhances athletic performance rather than diminishes it. Then this new fad called the "paleo diet" comes along, and the books it spawns start stacking up so fast that it feels like a conspiracy against everything vegan. Suddenly, meat-based, high-protein diets are "in" again. People once more embrace this improbable solution for long-term weight loss and good health. I even heard some people say, "I used to be vegan but now I've gone paleo." For a while, I felt like I was witnessing the invasion of the vegan snatchers, and it was enough to make me want to tear my thick vegan hair out! That is, until I discovered how much the paleo and vegan philosophies actually have in common

Whether their goal is to become healthy, lose weight, or simply eat more naturally, creative paleos have developed a cuisine to be reckoned with by using unrefined foods. And like any good thing, this eating style attracts others—paleo newbies who are either taking the full plunge or keeping their current diets and assimilating parts of the paleo philosophy. Like so many others, vegans are finding that with a few adjustments (including sidestepping the meat, of course), the paleo way of eating can add to the quality that's already on their plates.

WHAT IS A PALEO DIET?

Imagine this is the Paleolithic era. You emerge from your cave midmorning, charged with the responsibility of getting some food on the slab *pronto*. So will it be hunting or gathering today? Talk about a no-brainer! Even if you do spot an animal, catching and killing it would be anything but a cakewalk. Ah, but foraging. You're an expert at that. Leafy vegetables, grasses, berries, nuts—they're all yours for the taking, and these foods will sustain your family.

If only those cave folk knew the story today! Many of the dietary habits that were defined by their place and time are precisely the habits some modern paleos choose and can't live without. Naturally, current-day paleos have more options than our ancient relatives had. Here's a basic idea of what a modern paleo menu calls for:

- Whole, unprocessed foods
- Lean meats (from grass-fed or free-range animals) and seafood
- Low-carbohydrate foods that are high in fiber and potassium
- Healthy fats
- No grains, legumes, potatoes, dairy products, added salt, refined sugar, or refined vegetable oils

The Paleo Point of View

We all know processed foods lack sufficient nutrition compared with whole foods. What they *don't* lack are a bunch of additives and preservatives. So paleos are right on that point; refined foods are just a bum deal. Vegans may also feel that way about meat, but paleos stand their ground here, because a diet that includes lean meats, healthy fats, and fewer carbs is known to help in dropping pounds in the short run. And let's face it, a lot of people want that.

Now for the F-word. Fats are certainly necessary for us, but what we're seeing today is *trans*-fat mania. Margarine and other refined vegetable oils are full of the stuff, and if hearts could speak, they'd be shouting at us to knock it off! As for omega fats, the paleo diet instructs us to significantly decrease our omega-6 fatty acid intake, particularly from oils, such as corn and safflower oils. The paleo diet also encourages eating more foods high in omega-3 fatty acids, such as fish, so we can bring these fats into the same healthy ratio that Paleolithic people likely experienced. It's simple: too much omega-6 promotes the chronic diseases that omega-3 helps suppress. Vegans have a good source of omega-3 fatty acids in nuts and seeds, especially chia seeds, flaxseeds, and walnuts, and therefore never need to consume fish oil to get this essential fat.

Let's turn our attention to grains, legumes, and potatoes, which are the kind of "optional cheats" I talk about for vegans. These certainly are natural foods, and you might think a paleo would welcome them. But because they are the products of agriculture and can be difficult for some people to digest, the typical paleo passes on them. But that's not to say paleos aren't keen on other high-fiber, high-potassium foods, such as artichokes, bananas, and broccoli, to name a few. After all, fiber helps regulate cholesterol and blood sugar levels, and potassium is no slouch either. Just try running your kidneys or firing up a few nerves without enough of that baby in the tank!

That brings us to added salt and refined sugar. Most of us don't have to be given reasons for eliminating, or at least seriously decreasing, these little devils from our diets. An excess of sodium in the body is a time bomb for many people. Cutting out table salt while adding foods high in potassium helps to defuse this danger; otherwise, the body's natural acid levels get out of whack, and all sorts of disorders and diseases can set in. Refined sugar, which has no vitamins, minerals, or fiber, is another ticket to illness that nobody should be traveling on.

Benefits of Paleo Diets

Like other high-protein diets, paleo diets help people lose weight fast, which is a big reason they're so popular. Also, many health benefits are linked to eliminating processed foods—including the refined carbohydrates that contribute to obesity—and eating only whole, nutrient-dense foods in their natural state. These benefits include improved insulin response, a better acid–alkaline balance, and in-sync electrolytes.

People who are very active, including professional athletes, get certain advantages from the paleo diet too. In fact, certain well-known athletes praise the results they're getting from paleo diets that combine high protein, healthy fats, and minimal carbs. This is because, after adapting, the body switches from carbs to fat as its main fuel source during strenuous activity, conserving its glucose stores as much as possible. The kicker is that athletic performance may remain the same—or even improve. But also note that there are plenty of plant-guzzling athletes who have super performances on diets composed of 60–80 percent complex carbs. In fact, Kenyan marathoners report that their diets fall in this range.

Flexibility of Paleo Diets

Paleo diets aren't as strict as you might think, and people do tweak them to fit their needs. Here's an adapted list of notable allowances and recommendations from three popular versions of the paleo diet. There's no need for you to analyze or evaluate these choices. I just want to give you an idea of how different the interpretations can be.

VERSION ONE:

- Less emphasis on lean meats and more on grass-fed, free-range meats or meats and fish caught in the wild
- Relatively limited eating of fruits and nuts for people who want to lose weight
- Consumption of some starchy vegetables, such as yams and sweet potatoes, but limited consumption if weight gain is a concern

VERSION TWO:

- Emphasis on plant-based foods as the primary component
- Consumption of animal fats, such as butter, lard, and tallow
- Moderate consumption of dairy products

VERSION THREE:

- Raw vegetables and fruits, cooked vegetables, and meat or fish (all in equal portions)
- No more than four to five servings of fruit per day
- Occasional cheese or unsweetened yogurt

Although most paleos welcome "optional cheats," grains and legumes are apparently just too taboo to make it onto even one of these lists. Some paleos do consume a small amount of grains. Most avoid them, though, believing certain health issues result, at least in part, from mainstream agricultural practices. But the paleo tolerance for cheating is precisely what opens the door to vegans.

"CHEATING" YOUR WAY TO SUCCESS

A common characteristic of paleo diets is the concept of "cheating," which simply means eating some foods that aren't typically accepted as paleo. The authors of paleo books understand that most people would find it extremely difficult, if not impossible, to follow a paleo diet completely. So they encourage a little cheating based on individual needs and desires. Some paleo authors allow up to 15 percent of meals to contain cheat foods, whereas others go as far as 20 percent.

Paleo authors emphasize the importance of making cheats the exception, not the rule. The paleo concept allows occasional cheating so paleos get to taste some of the foods they miss the most, instead of jumping ship and losing the overall benefits of the diet. The point is to ease the feeling of deprivation, and after a while, some people find they don't need to cheat at all. Paleo authors encourage readers not to stress about perfection, to stay on course, and to accept an 80 percent success rate. After all, there are myriad pressures, distractions, and logistical challenges inherent in modern paleo living. Cheating 20 percent of the time leaves a lot of wiggle room—and for vegans, a lot of room to include grains and legumes.

What does a cheat look like in practical terms? Let's say you eat breakfast, lunch, and dinner every day (that's twenty-one meals per week). Cheating 20 percent of the time would allow you to "cheat" for about four of those meals. So, four times per week your lunches or dinners could include unrestricted grains and legumes, which you wouldn't eat the rest of the time. Alternatively, cheat foods could constitute about 20 percent of each, or many, of your meals.

Sensible Indulgences

Typical paleo cheats might be a slice of pizza or a milkshake, but I've also seen descriptions of some atypical cheats that involved all-out binges—including not only foods that are not on the traditional paleo spectrum but also alcohol. Whatever else our Paleolithic ancestors might have done to take the edge off, I like to believe that they didn't squander their limited resources on getting plastered!

If you occasionally enjoy a glass of wine, however, many paleos will toast with you. The use of wine, either for drinking or cooking, is acceptable as long as it's reasonable and moderate. Just be aware that although many studies have associated moderate wine drinking with good heart health, it's important for women to know that alcohol consumption has been linked to increased breast cancer risk.

While cheating allows us to indulge ourselves, we should choose sensible indulgences. Like a paleo diet, a vegan diet can allow for some flexibility. Most vegans would consider it "cheating" to accept a delicious dessert (maybe a piece of birthday cake) or other treat that, for whatever reason, isn't a part of their everyday repertoire. It's up to the individual to decide what's sensible.

Desirable Cheats

I would say that eating grains and legumes is certainly an acceptable cheat for vegans who want to incorporate paleo principles. I would even say these foods are *desirable* cheats because they provide fiber, B-complex vitamins, and many other benefits. For instance, beans, which are a good source of protein, iron, calcium, potassium, and magnesium, don't contribute to a spike in blood glucose levels and can help in reversing diabetes.

Paleos disapprove of grains and legumes largely because these foods have high levels of lectins, a kind of protein that can bind to cell membranes. What paleos fail to realize, though, is that soaking, fermenting, and sprouting significantly decrease lectin toxicity, and proper cooking generally destroys it. So if you soak dried beans for many hours, change the water often, and cook the beans well, you'll effectively deactivate the lectins while freeing up the nutrients.

Peas, quinoa, and wild rice are recommended in some paleo interpretations, so why not create your own interpretation and include the grains and legumes you like most? You could also include cacao, a healthful indulgence that's appropriate for both paleos and vegans. And why stop there? Combining cacao with fruits and nuts is right up the paleo-vegan alley. Fruits bring a lot to the table. Eating them with other foods, or just by themselves, can help curb the desire for desserts, because it's relatively easy to tame a sweet tooth by replacing added sugars with the natural sweetness of fruits. Consider adding dates to some dishes to satisfy the craving for something sweet. Just remember that dates, like any dried fruit, are high in sugar content as well as calories. Unless you're engaged in serious athletic training, keep your consumption of dried fruits at a reasonable level.

PALEO MEETS VEGAN

Vegans may think there's no place for them in the paleo universe, but take heart—there is a way to fit in! While it's true that standard paleo diets center around meat and fish, many similarities to vegan diets remain. For instance, even though most paleos and vegans have different reasons for avoiding dairy products, both groups know that calcium from plant sources is more easily absorbed by the body than calcium from dairy.

Vegans can also rejoice in the paleo's pantry-stocking strategy, which calls for fresh, nonperishable food items that are free of additives and preservatives, antibiotics, and pesticides. And paleos are in favor of buying from local producers whenever possible, which is something we can all get behind. Paleo cookbook authors are also spot on in suggesting we use all our senses when shopping—like touching and smelling produce and allowing ourselves to gravitate toward attractive colors in the produce aisle. What vegan would have it otherwise?

So. Paleo *and* vegan. Both diets stress the benefits of fresh fruits and vegetables, warn against processed foods, and generally support our health and well-being. Both aim to help people develop a nutrition plan that works. And I aim to show you how you can adopt a paleo diet while still sticking to your vegan principles. It's my sincere hope that the recipes and information in this book help you on this journey.

CHAPTER TWO

The Paleo-Style Vegan Diet

Paleo and vegan eating styles are alike when it comes to avoiding processed foods and sticking with what Mother Nature likely had in mind for optimal nutrition. If we look beyond the few aspects that make the two dietary styles different, we can see that an appealing array of fruits, vegetables, and other foods blend deliciously on the paleo-vegan plate. Let's consider what these diets have in common.

NUTS AND SEEDS

Humans have been eating nuts and seeds since the dawn of time. Historically, these foods often provided a source of sustenance during winter because they could be stored easily. As hunter-gatherers, our ancient relatives most likely subsisted on what was available nearby and met their protein needs by accumulating and consuming these tiny but mighty morsels.

Nuts and seeds often get a bad rap because they're high in fat. But Mother Nature, in her infinite wisdom, encapsulated them in hard shells that often take time to open. This cracking and opening procedure slows down consumption and discourages excessive caloric intake unless, of course, you liberate the little buggers from their shells all at once and start devouring them!

FRUITS

There's no question that fruits were part of the original paleo pickings. For instance, archaeological digs in northern Israel have revealed ancient figs, olives, pears, and plums. In addition, remnants of grapes from seven million years ago were found in Tennessee. Remains found at other ancient sites confirmed the early consumption of fruit, so we can reasonably assume that a Paleolithic person wouldn't have set up shop where fruits weren't abundant. Today, the list of preferred paleo fruits is quite extensive, with dark berries claiming the top position.

COLORFUL VEGETABLES

Green vegetables are the powerhouses of a vegan diet, and the paleo diet follows suit by including a wide variety of these essentials. In addition, both diets call for foods rich in antioxidants, which are plant chemicals that protect against such illnesses as cancer, cardiovascular disease, and diabetes. In fact, antioxidants combat inflammation and oxidative stress, which can lead to many kinds of degenerative, chronic disease. The easiest way to load up on these healthful plant chemicals is to choose colorful vegetables, because antioxidants, such as anthocyanidins, carotenoids, catechins, and flavones, give vegetables their hues.

Just like us, modern vegetables are different from their progenitors. This is because, even before the official dawn of agriculture, vegetables were "genetically altered." This simply means that in Paleolithic times, early humans encouraged the best-tasting seedlings to partner up with each other. For example, brassica vegetables, such as broccoli, Brussels sprouts, cabbage, kale, and kohlrabi, are all thought to have evolved from one prehistoric plant.

HEALTHY FATS

Our paleo ancestors probably didn't stomp on olives or other foods to squeeze out their oils. Rather, Paleolithic people in the Middle East, where civilization may have originated and where olives have long been abundant, probably just foraged and ate olives in their natural state.

All plant-based foods contain some amount of fat, even if only a minuscule amount, and paleos and vegans agree that these naturally occurring fats are healthy. However, when it comes to rendered, extracted, and added fats, the recommended kinds and quantities vary across interpretations. The motley paleo diets present interesting contradictions and paradoxes. For example, some authors include butter, lard, and even tallow on their lists of healthy fats. Of course, my paleo-vegan interpretation doesn't include these fats. Consistent with my vegan bent, I'll stick with plant-based foods to get nutritious fats and oils.

We all care about our weight, so of course it's wise to pay attention to calorie intake. Maybe our paleo ancestors ran around enough to get away with consuming a high percentage of fat, but most of us—except, perhaps, marathoners and sumo wrestlers—need to keep some distance from those nut-butter balls! Fats, including oils, have 9 calories per gram, versus 4 calories for proteins and 4 calories for carbohydrates. Adding oils can pile on the calories faster than you can devour a butter-laden potato. Just one tablespoon of butter weighs 14 grams, which equals 102 calories. To get flavor without the fat, you can skip the butter and top a baked potato with chopped green onions and tomatoes, sliced almonds, and steamed broccoli florets.

By avoiding added fat, you can eat loads of fruits and vegetables and not fret much about calories. You can also enjoy raw, unsalted nuts and seeds, particularly if you have to shell them. Taking time to remove the shells gives your brain the needed fifteen to twenty minutes to get the signal that your stomach is filling up. Not only that, you won't need to eat a lot, because whole nuts and seeds are packed with nutrients, which makes them real hunger busters.

RAW VERSUS COOKED FOODS

A traditional paleo diet dovetails nicely with a raw vegan diet, which focuses on whole, unprocessed foods as they're found in nature. Like paleo diets and whole-food, plant-based diets in general, raw vegan diets have been shown to protect against cancer, heart disease, and diabetes. They can help you lose weight too.

If you're into the raw vegan approach, you can blend, sprout, or dehydrate certain foods to liven up your dishes. Not surprisingly, raw enthusiasts turn away from processed foods—other than the occasional use of extracted oils, vinegar, tamari, and a few natural sweeteners—and rely primarily on fresh produce and nuts. Sprouted legumes and whole grains are used occasionally in a raw vegan diet. For example, wheat berries are soaked to make whole-grain breads and treats or fermented to make a culture for raw nut cheeses. However, grains can be eliminated altogether.

Raw vegan diets nix refined carbohydrates and boost intakes of healthy phytochemicals, just as traditional paleo diets do. They also tend to be low in sodium and harmful fats. In addition, they don't contain the dangerous substances that form when foods are cooked at high temperatures. These by-products have mind-bending names, such as advanced glycation end products, heterocyclic amines, and polycyclic aromatic hydrocarbons.

There's discussion in the paleo community about how the process of cooking foods makes some nutrients easier to absorb; this is known as increased bioavailability. However, because people who follow a raw vegan diet consume such a wide variety of fresh produce, their diets contain enough nutrients to make up for any absorption problems. That said, anyone who consumes a raw vegan diet should include some sprouted legumes from time to time, because sprouts are lower in calories than nuts, which can be overdone as a primary protein source. Sprouting can improve the quality of protein in legumes and make it more digestible. Sprouting also helps to remove the enzyme inhibitors that keep proteins from being assimilated. Lentils and mung beans can be sprouted and eaten raw; other legumes, such as garbanzo beans and kidney beans, can be sprouted, but the sprouts must be cooked before they are eaten.

If you have a raw vegan diet, be sure to supplement with vitamin B_{12}. In fact, supplementation is a good idea for anyone, vegan or not. Unless you live in the tropics and get good sun exposure year-round, you'll also want to supplement with a vegan form of vitamin D.

GETTING THE PROTEIN YOU NEED

s a vegan athlete, I hear the same question whenever I lecture: "Where do you get your protein?" Usually, I flex my biceps and say, "Does it look like I have a protein deficiency? Does anyone here know somebody who has a protein deficiency?" No one raises a hand.

Then I ask, "Do you know anyone who has heart disease, diabetes, or cancer?" Many hands go up. "That's where we should be focusing our energy and resources," I tell my audiences, "on correcting these genuine, serious health problems."

FOODS BOTH VEGANS AND PALEOS CAN ENJOY

Let's look at how much overlap there is between paleo and vegan foods. There are certainly enough options to keep you happy, healthy, and full of energy. Here's a composite of the approved foods on some popular paleo shopping lists.

NUTS AND SEEDS

Almonds	Hazelnuts	Pecans	Pistachios	Sesame seeds	Walnuts
Brazil nuts	Macadamia nuts	Pine nuts	Pumpkin seeds	Sunflower seeds	

PREFERRED FRUITS

Blackberries	Blueberries	Boysenberries	Cranberries	Gooseberries	Raspberries

OTHER FRUITS

Apple	Fig	Kiwifruit	Nectarine	Pear	Rhubarb
Apricot	Goji berries	Lemon	Orange	Persimmon	Star fruit
Banana	Grapefruit	Lime	Papaya	Pineapple	Strawberries
Cantaloupe	Grapes	Lychee	Passion fruit	Plum	Tangerine
Cherries	Guava	Mango	Peach	Pomegranate	Watermelon
Coconut	Honeydew melon				

SPICES AND HERBS

Anise	Chiles, ground	Cumin	Mint	Paprika	Sage
Basil	Cilantro	Dill	Mustard seeds	Parsley	Tarragon
Black pepper	Cinnamon	Fennel	Nutmeg	Peppermint	Thyme
Cayenne	Cloves	Ginger	Oregano	Rosemary	Turmeric
Chiles, dried	Coriander seeds				

VEGETABLES

Artichoke	Broccoli	Chile	Green beans	Olives	Sea vegetables
Arugula	Broccoli rabe	Collard greens	Jerusalem artichoke	Onion	Spinach
Asparagus	Brussels sprouts	Cucumber	Jicama	Parsnip	Squash
Avocado	Cabbage	Eggplant	Kale	Pumpkin	Swiss chard
Beets	Carrot	Endive	Kohlrabi	Purslane	Tomato
Beet greens	Cauliflower	Fennel	Leek	Radish	Turnip greens
Bell pepper	Celery	Fiddlehead fern	Mushrooms	Romaine lettuce	Watercress
Bok choy	Celery root	Garlic	Mustard greens	Rutabaga	

FOODS FOR MODERATE CONSUMPTION

Amaranth	Cassava	Potato	Sweet potato	Wild rice	Yam
Buckwheat	Hempseeds	Quinoa	Taro		

HEALTHY FATS AND OILS TO BE USED SPARINGLY

Avocado oil	Coconut oil	Olive oil	Sesame oil	Walnut oil
Coconut milk	Macadamia oil	Palm oil, unprocessed		

OTHER ITEMS

Coffee	Dark chocolate	Tamari	Tea	Vinegar

Protein Sources

Vegans and paleos both know that protein is provided by energy-giving nuts and seeds, but not everyone realizes that all vegetables contain some protein. Still, rather than relying only on vegetables, nuts, and seeds for protein, many vegans tap other desirable protein sources, such as grains and legumes. Since vegans don't eat meat like paleos do, this is where they can take advantage of the paleo tolerance for cheating. In paleo terms, cheating means selecting up to 20 percent of your foods from the list of foods that aren't paleo. For vegans, this includes eating beans (especially high-protein, whole-soy edamame and tempeh) for additional protein. If this fits your diet, you could have a meal with beans four times per week and still be on track with paleo.

What's the paleo enthusiast's beef against grains and legumes? In a nutshell, most paleos believe that Paleolithic people didn't eat these foods. Therefore, most modern paleos choose not to eat them. They point to genetically modified grain and legume crops, specifically corn, soy, and wheat, and claim these modifications cause health problems. While the jury is still out on this, an easy solution is to buy organic grains and legumes and avoid genetically modified foods altogether.

In addition, some paleos are concerned that the enzyme inhibitors that make beans inedible in their raw state may interfere with digestion. However, cooking beans until they're soft destroys these inhibitors. Sprouting beans is another way to decrease the amount of enzyme inhibitors, and steaming sprouted beans will eliminate even more of these inhibitors. If you decide to try sprouting, be aware that some sprouts, such as sprouted garbanzo beans, kidney beans, and soybeans, shouldn't be eaten raw.

People who have problems eating legumes even after they're cooked aren't reacting to enzyme inhibitors but to something else. The culprits here are really the natural sugars in beans. Soaking beans for eight hours and then cooking them well can greatly reduce their sugar content. So can adding a piece of kombu, a sea vegetable, to beans while they cook.

Another source of protein is hempseeds, which contain all the essential amino acids. The jury is still out on whether hempseeds act more like nuts or grains during digestion, but if you don't experience any adverse effects, why worry about it? Including whole hempseeds or ground hempseeds can really boost the protein in your diet, which can be especially helpful for athletes.

The grain-like seeds amaranth, buckwheat, and quinoa also contain protein, although they're primarily carbohydrate. Some paleo proponents don't recommend these pseudograins because they believe these foods react in the gut like grains. But you're the boss. If any of these foods appeal to you, save them for your optional cheats.

How Much Protein Is Enough?

Some experts say vegans need less protein than meat eaters because plant protein is more easily absorbed by the body, whereas others claim vegans need slightly more protein than meat eaters. As a personal trainer and running coach, I don't believe one size fits all. How much protein an individual needs depends on multiple factors, including age, gender, body weight, activity level, and health status. Black-and-white thinking just doesn't work here. That's why the "correct" amounts of protein needed for everyday life and athletic competition continue to be so widely debated. To simplify things, I'll stick with the Goldilocks model—the answer is "not too much, not too little, but enough." A well-rounded vegan diet that includes a colorful rotation of nuts, seeds, and vegetables, along with some legumes (particularly sprouted legumes) and grains, will undoubtedly provide enough protein.

TABLE 1. Vegan protein sources

FOOD	AMOUNT	PROTEIN (IN GRAMS)
Tempeh	1 cup	30
Lentils	1 cup	18
Spirulina, dried	1 ounce	16
Beans (black, garbanzo, and pinto), cooked	1 cup	15
Almonds	2 ounces	12
Tofu, firm	4 ounces	11
Hempseeds	3 tablespoons	10
Almond butter	2 tablespoons	8
Quinoa, cooked	1 cup	8
Broccoli, cooked	1 large stalk	7
Spinach, cooked	1 cup	5.3
Peas, cooked	1 cup	5
Sunflower seeds	1 ounce	5
Sweet potato, cooked	1 cup	3
Avocado	1 ounce	1
Kale, cooked	1 cup	1

Not satisfied with Goldilocks? Fine. Let's make that little mathematician in you happy. According to the USDA, the daily protein recommendations for adults who are somewhat sedentary are 56 grams for men and 46 grams for women. For vegans, the recommendations are higher. Nutrition experts estimate that vegans with average activity levels need at least 0.8 gram of protein per day for every kilogram of body weight. That comes to about 62 grams of protein per day for a person who weighs 150 pounds (68 kilograms). It's hard to visualize what 62 grams of protein represents in the daily diet. To simplify, a useful guideline is to fill one-third of your plate with protein.

What if you're an athlete, like I am? For endurance and weight training, the recommended daily protein intake varies widely, from 1.3 grams per kilogram of body weight for endurance athletes to 1.9 grams per kilogram of body weight for strength training. Without enough protein, the body begins "cannibalizing" muscle for energy, so the lean muscle mass we're trying to build and maintain winds up getting broken down and used for fuel.

GETTING THE CALCIUM YOU NEED

After I tell audiences where I get my protein, they always ask, "Where do you get your calcium?" I explain that I get it from a variety of plant-based sources. Usually, after making that statement, I can see at least a few incredulous faces in the crowd. That's when I start singing the praises of calcium-rich vegetables, such as bok choy, collard greens, and kale.

Besides being necessary for the bones, calcium is important for proper nerve and muscle function as well as blood clotting. If the body parts responsible for such functions are calcium deprived, they'll "borrow" calcium from the bones, which can increase fraction risk and cause other problems. Of course, most people, unless they're paleos or vegans, rely on dairy products for calcium. However, dairy-based calcium is associated with some serious health problems, including fractures and cancer. Interestingly, the United States has among the highest rates of milk consumption *and* osteoporosis, and one prestigious, long-term study even found that women who frequently consumed dairy products broke more bones than those who rarely consumed them. Furthermore, cow's milk contains insulin-like growth factor 1, which is believed by some researchers to cause cancer cell growth in humans.

Nature provides enough nutrition in other foods so that all mammals, once weaned, never need to drink any kind of milk. Although humans developed a taste for animal milks and the foods made from them 10,000 to 7,000 years ago, not all primal peoples were able to digest these foods. And the situation hasn't changed

TABLE 2. High-calcium plant-based foods

FOOD	AMOUNT	CALCIUM (IN MILLIGRAMS)
Hempseeds	8 ounces	460
Almond milk	8 ounces	450
Blackstrap molasses	2 tablespoons	400
Collard greens, cooked	1 cup	357
Orange juice (calcium-fortified)	8 ounces	350
Commercial soy yogurt, plain	6 ounces	300
Turnip greens, cooked	1 cup	249
Tofu (processed with calcium sulfate)	4 ounces	200–420
Soy, rice, or oat milk (commercial, calcium-fortified, plain)	8 ounces	200–300
Tempeh	1 cup	184
Kale, cooked	1 cup	179
Chia seeds	1 ounce	177
Bok choy, cooked	1 cup	158
Mustard greens, cooked	1 cup	152
Okra, cooked	1 cup	135
Tofu (processed with nigari)	4 ounces	130–400
Tahini	2 tablespoons	128
Almond butter	2 tablespoons	111
Almonds, whole	¼ cup	94
Broccoli, cooked	1 cup	62

much over all these years. Look around today and you'll see that countless people are still affected by allergies, bloating, and lactose intolerance, all of which are related to their inability to digest milk. Fortunately, more people are discovering that calcium is abundant in plant sources and that the body is better at absorbing calcium from plant-based foods. In fact, many people are amazed at how much better they feel after dumping the dairy.

Calcium Sources

While paleos and vegans don't always agree on where to get their calcium, both acknowledge its importance in the diet. Paleos, for example, may rely on fish as a source of calcium, while vegans count on calcium-rich legumes. Neither finds the other's choice appealing. However, paleos and vegans alike share excellent sources of calcium in such foods as green leafy vegetables, nuts, and seeds.

On the previous page is a list of vegan foods that are high in calcium. Tofu, soy yogurt, and the soy, rice, and oat milks aren't paleo, but everything else, including the lightly processed hemp and almond milks, *is* paleo. The non-paleo items could be part of your 20 percent cheat.

GETTING THE IRON AND VITAMIN B_{12} YOU NEED

A udiences don't often ask me where I get my iron and vitamin B_{12}—but they should. Iron deficiency is the most common nutritional deficiency in the world. As a key component of red blood cells, iron is essential in the transport of oxygen throughout the body and the removal of carbon dioxide. Because we need to keep these blood cells healthy, our bodies require vitamin B_{12}, which also keeps our nervous system healthy and aids in the synthesis and regulation of DNA.

To get iron and vitamin B_{12}, vegans have to look beyond the animal-based foods that supply both so readily. Because iron from plant-based foods isn't absorbed as easily as iron from meat, vegans should aim for 1.8 times as much iron as the recommended intake for meat eaters. Vegan women of childbearing age should get 32.4 milligrams of iron per day, and they generally need an extra 30 to 45 milligrams each month due to the iron lost during menstruation. Other vegan adults need 14.4 milligrams of iron per day, and athletes need a little more because of increased oxygen demands.

Vitamin C and foods high in citric acid, such as citrus fruits, increase the absorption of iron. In general, it's a good practice to combine these foods with iron-rich foods. Because most vegans get more than enough vitamin C from eating so many fruits and vegetables, the iron we need can get right in and do its work. However, consuming certain items, such as tea, coffee, and calcium supplements can hinder iron absorption. So if you're susceptible to iron deficiency, avoid these items one hour before and one hour after consuming iron-rich foods.

Vitamin B_{12} is produced by bacteria. Including it in your diet requires special attention because it doesn't occur naturally in plants; even if bacteria are present in the soil used to grow the plants, fruits and vegetables aren't reliable sources of vitamin B_{12}. Meat eaters get most of their B_{12} by eating animal products, but everyone is at risk of having problems absorbing B_{12} as they age. Although the body requires only small amounts of vitamin B_{12}, the consequences of not getting enough include irreversible nervous system damage. The average adult requires 2.4 micrograms of vitamin B_{12} per day.

TABLE 3. Plant-based sources of iron

FOOD	AMOUNT	IRON (IN MILLIGRAMS)
Soybeans, cooked	1 cup	8.8
Blackstrap molasses	2 tablespoons	7.2
Spinach, cooked	1 cup	6.8
Lentils, cooked	1 cup	6.6
Tofu	4 ounces	6.4
Tempeh	1 cup	4.8
Lima beans, cooked	1 cup	4.5
Kidney beans, cooked	1 cup	4.2
Swiss chard, cooked	1 cup	4
Beans (black or pinto), cooked	1 cup	3.6
Turnip greens, cooked	1 cup	3.2
Quinoa, cooked	1 cup	2.8
Beet greens, cooked	1 cup	2.7
Tahini	2 tablespoons	2.7
Cashews	¼ cup	2.1
Bok choy, cooked	1 cup	1.8

Iron and Vitamin B_{12} Sources

Good sources of iron are plentiful for vegans. For example, green leafy vegetables, (especially cooked spinach) pack a nice punch, as do grains and legumes. Soaking, fermenting, and sprouting break down the phytate compounds in grains and legumes, and as a result, iron and other minerals from these sources can be more easily absorbed. Substances in onions and garlic also help increase iron absorption from grains and legumes, so add them often to your bean and grain dishes. Nuts (particularly cashews) and dried fruits (especially apricots and raisins) also provide iron.

To get a reliable vegan source of vitamin B_{12}, you either have to consume foods fortified with B_{12} (such as some breakfast cereals, some plant milks, certain brands of nutritional yeast, and some soy products) or take a supplement. Two options, that's all—and you absolutely must choose one of them.

DEFINING "WILD" AND "EXOTIC" FOR VEGANS

Paleos champion the consumption of exotic game meats. Many paleos who don't have access to such meats eat free-range or grass-fed meats instead. Wild and exotic foods for vegans, on the other hand, are much easier to find. Such foods may be only as far away as your local farmers' market. Wild mushrooms are the first obvious vegan food that comes to mind. Books abound on how to safely forage or discover edible wild mushrooms and other plants in your own backyard. Dozens of varieties that are safe to eat have been identified. But if you're concerned about safety or don't have access to wild plants and mushrooms in your own surroundings, an increasing number of grocery stores and ethnic markets are selling a variety of these foods.

If you go foraging, the best way to correctly identify wild mushrooms, or any edible wild plant for that matter, is to forage with an expert. It's obviously imperative to distinguish safe mushrooms from poisonous ones. Don't assume all mushrooms found together are the same, and don't pick mushrooms that are too young because they may not yet have the necessary identifying characteristics (mushrooms look different at different stages of development). Try tasting a small amount to make sure you've identified the species correctly and to minimize any reaction if the identification was incorrect. Also, as with any wild food, avoid foraging close to industrialized or polluted areas, because chemicals and metals can leach into the soil and plants.

Wild mushrooms make excellent broths and sauces for soups, vegetables, and stand-alone main courses. Some common varieties found at stores are chanterelle, enoki, morel, oyster, and shiitake. Less common varieties with particularly odd names are bay bolete, cauliflower fungus, deer shield, ear fungus (also called wood ear and black fungus), lawyer's wig (also known as shaggy inkcap), and mosaic puffball. Who made up these names? The creative, brave souls who were the first to taste them and didn't drop dead!

Another popular food to forage is dandelion greens, which are also commonly found in grocery stores. Dandelions were brought to the United States by colonists who wanted to make tea from the roots and edible flowers. However, other parts of the plant have gained popularity. The leaves are delicious in salads, juices, or cooked dishes. The buds can also be used in salads. Older greens are more bitter than younger greens, but the slightly bitter taste can be neutralized with vinegar, and the greens can be cooked just like kale or spinach. Dandelion greens are high in calcium and have long been associated with healing powers in the macrobiotic diet.

If you forage dandelion greens, beware of the backyard variety. If your yard has ever been treated for dandelions, you may not want to eat the greens. Be sure to know the land well. Never pick dandelions by railroad tracks or telephone poles, because chemicals can leach from the treated wood used to make them. Also, wherever you pick dandelions or other plants, make sure you have the legal right to do so.

Other edible wild plants include burdock, cattail, chickweed, chicory, clover, daisies, fireweed, garlic mustard, miner's lettuce, nettles, and lamb's-quarters. In fact, lamb's-quarters is high in protein and outranks broccoli, collard greens, and spinach as a nutritional powerhouse.

The list of plants to forage goes on and on. Wild asparagus, which is a great source of potassium, thiamine, vitamin B_6, and vitamin C, has a much thinner stalk than the grocery-store variety. It's a delicious vegetable that you can either cook or eat raw. And there are more than four hundred types of edible grasses, wheatgrass being the most recognized and popular for its health benefits. Then there's amaranth, which is native to the Americas but found on most continents. All parts of the amaranth plant are edible, but the spines that appear on some leaves aren't palatable. Although they're not poisonous, amaranth leaves do contain oxalic acid and may contain large amounts of nitrates if grown in nitrate-rich soil. It's best to boil the leaves to remove these substances, even though you *can* eat the plant raw, if desired. And finally, sea vegetables of all kinds are also edible, but ideally they should be rinsed in fresh water before being consumed. Adding them to a soup or salad, or just cooking them with a little soy sauce or seasoning them with a dollop of miso after cooking is a quick and flavorful way to quickly pack in a variety of nutrients.

If wild and exotic plants aren't at your fingertips, don't worry. Most of the conventional fruits and vegetables at your local store or market will do.

SOLUTIONS FOR ACTIVE PEOPLE AND PALEO-VEGAN ATHLETES

People who are very active, and especially athletes, have dietary needs above and beyond those of the average person. Since 2006, I've placed in dozens of 5,000-kilometer or longer races in my age group, and I know from experience that if I don't fill my tank with the proper types and quantities of nutrients, I'll be running on empty faster than you can say "last place." Of course, as a serious competitor, I never let that happen. I pay attention to my body at all times and make sure I give it what it needs in order to perform at its highest level. And if I'm racing neck and neck with someone toward the finish line, you can bet that person routinely does the same. Our needs may be different because our bodies are different, but we both know the score on our respective situations.

Experimenting with Carbohydrate Intake

If you're not an athlete but have a relatively active lifestyle and want to explore the paleo diet, you might start by trying one of the most basic steps—increasing your protein intake while lowering your carbohydrates—to see how you feel. Basically, your body will be learning how to use dietary fat (from foods such as avocados, nuts, olives, and healthier plant oils in moderation) instead of carbohydrates as its immediate source of fuel. Some bodies make this adjustment easier than others due to several factors, including genetics and metabolism. The only way for you to know how your body will react to such a change is to put it to the test. Because you're trying to determine whether you can perform as well, or even better, on fewer carbohydrates, I suggest one of two approaches:

- If grains and legumes aren't central to your diet and you want to try the strict paleo route, eliminate grains and legumes, as well as refined sugars.
- If your diet depends on grains and legumes, cut back on them significantly and eliminate all refined sugars. Of course, be sure to get enough nutrients from other foods.

Stick to your chosen course for at least a few weeks to see how this modification affects your energy level. If you find that you're moody, sluggish, or experiencing any negative effects that might be related to this diet change, try restoring some carbohydrates—while keeping your other paleo habits the same—to see if that helps. If your energy level improves, experiment with your carbohydrate intake until you can confidently determine the right amount of daily carbs for your particular body. Always remember that respecting your body's wisdom should be the priority.

Let's assume that you need more carbs than the standard paleo diet recommends. Which sources should you choose? Besides eating more grains and legumes, you can consume a lot more fruit, either whole or blended into smoothies. Eat squashes and sweet potatoes as well. Unlike regular potatoes, which aren't paleo-approved and don't offer much in terms of nutrients, sweet potatoes are loaded with nutrients and get a hearty paleo thumbs-up.

Carbohydrate Needs of Athletes

"Carbohydrate loading" typically refers to a strategy that many endurance athletes use. By loading up on carbs, they hope to maximize the storage of muscle glycogen so it can be readily converted into glucose. But athletes who eat a balanced vegan diet appropriate for their sport never need to engage in carbohydrate loading. Their glycogen fuel stores are always stocked and ready to go at a moment's notice.

The paleo diet makes certain exceptions for athletes, allowing quinoa, starchy tubers, and wild rice. (For non-athletes, these foods would qualify as "cheats.") These foods are already a regular part of many vegan athletes' diets, which makes it easy for vegans to adopt this paleo tenant. Given the special needs of athletes, paleos also recommend that those who require more carbohydrates consume only complex carbs, such as sweet potatoes and squashes.

Getting Enough Calories

Active and athletic people obviously have to make sure they get enough calories throughout the day so they don't run out of steam. Several high-performing vegan athletes reveal in their books that consuming copious amounts of nuts, seeds, and healthy fats is what keeps the pistons pumping. Because these athletes are calorie-burning machines, they need the extra calories these foods can deliver. They say that to be truly on top of their game, their bodies have to be in superb fat-burning shape.

Are you in excellent fat-burning shape? One indicator is that you don't feel hungry until at least one to two hours into your training. Hunger is the body's signal that it's almost finished burning carbs and ready to burn fat. If your carb intake is low, as paleo proponents would have it be, this switch occurs relatively quickly, and your fat reserves become instant fuel.

Regardless of whether you get your fuel from burning carbs or fat, the most important thing is to make sure your body has enough of whichever one you choose so that it doesn't start feeding on muscle. For endurance athletes, loss of muscle mass can decrease strength, power, and performance. This also explains why the longer someone is on a calorie-restricted diet, the more their overall metabolic rate, also known as the "set point," decreases. The body goes into "starvation mode," doing whatever is necessary to hang on to every bit of available fat in preparation for the "famine" to come.

Paleos commonly recommend that animal-based foods take up 30 to 50 percent of daily calories. But paleo experts who have a better overall understanding of athletes' needs say that this percentage is challenging and difficult to maintain. Why? Training for endurance sports puts a great burden on the body. The athlete is constantly in a state of recovery during intense training. Paleos suggest that eating low-glycemic or moderately glycemic fruits and vegetables may fit the bill for optimal recovery. And that's exactly what so many headline-grabbing vegan athletes report—plant-based foods actually enhance performance. (Naturally, there would be no winning performance without proper rest and recovery from previous stress on the body.)

How do these recommendations translate into practice? It doesn't mean consuming cabbage-and-bean soup for breakfast before a training run or some other demanding exercise. In fact, many non-vegan websites for athletes recommend eating complex yet easy-to-digest carbohydrates before exercising. This can mean different foods for different people. Many athletes do just fine for several hours on one-half cup of cooked old-fashioned oats with berries. Some athletes experience cramps after eating protein before exercise. There's no single formula for success here. It's simply a matter of learning to listen to your own body.

During long workouts, such as distance races, most people gain an advantage by consuming high-glycemic carbohydrates, such as sports drinks. If your activity doesn't last more than one hour, you shouldn't need extra carbs. But if you'll be out there longer, giving it all you've got, it's wise to gas up on the carbs as needed.

What to eat after intense physical activity is hardly debatable. It's common practice—and crucially important—to consume a good source of protein and carbohydrates between thirty and sixty minutes after exercise to help speed the recovery and rebuilding of muscles that have been stressed and slightly broken down from all your fervent efforts. Keep eating over the next few hours. Glucose-rich carbs will help a lot (once again, sweet potatoes to the rescue!) in the recovery process, so if you want pasta or bread, for instance, go for it. The goal is to replenish all that you just spent in the name of performance. Enjoy your carbs. Don't worry, paleos will pardon you.

For people who want instant calorie calculations at their fingertips, there are some superb smartphone apps that can tell you exactly how many net calories you have to "spend." To get this information, you must enter all the foods you eat at every meal and the amount of time you've spent running, walking, or whatever other exercise you've done that day. This technology makes it easy to keep track of your nutrient intake and can help you figure out what works best for you and whether your daily requirements are being met.

Paleo Exercise

It's no secret that whatever your diet, an appropriate exercise regimen is recommended for maintaining good health. Whether you already have such a regimen (of course I know *you* do, my fellow athlete!) or are interested in starting one, here's what paleos suggest:

- Engage in functional exercises (such as planks, push-ups, pull-ups, and squats, or exercises that mimic these motions).
- Sprint a few seconds per week.
- Safely lift heavy things for thirty to sixty minutes a day with one day of rest per week.
- Move at a slow to moderate pace for up to five hours per week.

The term "functional exercises" refers to a type of training that helps build strength through exercises that get us to move multiple muscles and joints in unison. Unlike the exercises carried out on gym machines, which target a narrow range of muscles, functional exercises are more holistic and designed to facilitate our movements and activities in everyday life. Accomplished vegan endurance athletes and others argue that we were born to run long distances, especially to outrun our predators. According to paleos, the emphasis should be on moving the body as naturally as possible. Whichever form of exercise you choose, just make sure you get enough rest to recover from your training.

CHAPTER THREE

at sunrise, gathering energy . . .

breakfast

Breakfast is the ideal time to eat cleansing and healing foods, as the body is primed to receive after a night's fasting. You can taste the health benefits in this fresh, pleasantly astringent treat.

spiced apple-a-day STARTER

MAKES 1 SERVING

1 **apple,** grated

¼ cup raw or toasted **pecans,** halved

Juice of ½ **lemon**

1 teaspoon ground **cinnamon**

Put all the ingredients in a small bowl and stir until well combined. Eat!

Per serving: 272 calories, 3 g protein, 20 g fat (2 g sat), 28 g carbohydrates, 2 mg sodium, 57 mg calcium, 7 g fiber

This morning pick-me-up will get any cave dweller going. The classic pineapple-coconut combination gets a boost of protein from the addition of hempseeds. Feel free to add more hempseeds if you wish; unlike protein powder, hempseeds are very light.

pineapple-coconut SMOOTHIE

MAKES 2 SERVINGS

2 cups diced **pineapple**

1½ cups **coconut water**

½ cup full-fat **coconut milk**

½ cup **hempseeds**

Put all the ingredients in a blender and process until smooth.

VARIATION: For an extra burst of flavor, add 1 tablespoon of chopped fresh ginger.

Per serving: 519 calories, 17 g protein, 30 g fat (10 g sat), 53 g carbohydrates, 49 mg sodium, 295 mg calcium, 5 g fiber

Nothing says "primal" like leafy greens and fruits, and this smoothie is a terrific way to start the day. It's low in fat, stimulating, and light enough to keep you alert.

kale, green apple, and lime SMOOTHIE

MAKES 1 SERVING

2 cups **coconut water,** plus more as needed

1 cup coarsely chopped **kale leaves**

1 **green apple,** cut into chunks

½ cup **hempseeds**

1 tablespoon freshly squeezed **lime juice**

Put all the ingredients in a blender and process until smooth. If the mixture is too thick, add a little more coconut water or plain water and process briefly.

Per serving: 519 calories, 24 g protein, 20 g fat (2 g sat), 56 g carbohydrates, 119 mg sodium, 154 mg calcium, 8 g fiber

A staple of Mesoamerican tribesmen, chia seeds are a potent combination of protein, essential fats, minerals, antioxidants, and soluble fiber. They also balance blood sugar and stave off hunger, making them the perfect breakfast food.

chia cereal WITH BANANA

MAKES 1 SERVING

1 cup **almond milk**

2 tablespoons **chia seeds**

½ teaspoon **vanilla extract**

1 **banana**, sliced

¼ teaspoon lightly crushed **cardamom seeds** (optional)

Put the almond milk in a small bowl. Add the chia seeds and vanilla extract and stir briskly for at least 1 minute to prevent the chia seeds from clumping. Cover and refrigerate for at least 20 minutes or up to 8 hours.

Just before serving, stir the chia seed mixture. Add the banana and optional cardamom and stir until well combined.

Per serving: 265 calories, 8 g protein, 9 g fat (0.3 g sat), 35 g carbohydrates, 151 mg sodium, 460 mg calcium, 14 g fiber ur Paleolithic ancestors would agree that there's nothing like a bowl of fresh berries first thing in the morning. Now you can take this perennial pleasure to a new level with a bowl of fresh berries in a sauce of puréed berries. Don't forget the lemon verbena, a pleasant-tasting herb that calms the digestive system and supports the nervous system.

mixed berries WITH BERRY PURÉE AND LEMON VERBENA

MAKES 4 SERVINGS

2½ cups **blueberries**

2½ cups **marionberries or blackberries** (see Foraging for Flavor)

2 cups **strawberries,** halved or quartered lengthwise

1 tablespoon **palm sugar** (optional)

2 cups **raspberries**

1 cup **blackberries**

1 cup **golden raspberries**

2 tablespoons coarsely chopped **lemon verbena leaves**

Put 1 cup of the blueberries, 1 cup of the marionberries, ½ cup of the strawberries, and the optional palm sugar in a blender. Process until smooth. Strain to remove any seeds and put in a medium bowl. Add the remaining 1½ cups of blueberries, 1½ cups of marionberries, and 1½ cups of strawberries along with the raspberries, blackberries, golden raspberries, and lemon verbena. Toss gently but thoroughly and serve at once.

Per serving: 200 calories, 4 g protein, 1 g fat (0.1 g sat), 52 g carbohydrates, 16 mg sodium, 95 mg calcium, 14 g fiber

OPTIONAL CHEAT: Although sugar is typically avoided in a strict paleo diet, a little extra sweetness now and then can greatly elevate flavors. Palm sugar is the most natural form of sugar available, and it has both a low glycemic index and a low fructose content.

FORAGING FOR FLAVOR

Marionberries are related to blackberries. They are dark like blackberries, but a bit sweeter, juicier, and more plump. Look for them at farm stands, natural food stores, or specialty markets in the summer. If they're not available, substitute with an equal quantity of fresh blackberries.

Fresh and dried fruits offer a bright start, and this combination is full of stimulating flavors, antioxidants, and cleansing compounds. Goji berries are rich in vitamin A and help promote eye health, which is an advantage for the modern-day hunter-gatherer.

mango, papaya, pineapple & kiwifruit WITH GOJI BERRIES AND MINT

MAKES 4 SERVINGS

1½ cups diced **mango**

1½ cups diced **papaya**

1½ cups diced **pineapple**

4 **kiwifruit,** peeled, quartered, and sliced about ¼-inch thick

½ cup dried **goji berries** (see Foraging for Flavor)

1 tablespoon freshly squeezed **lime juice**

½ teaspoon lightly crushed **cardamom seeds**

12 fresh **mint leaves**

Put the mango, papaya, pineapple, kiwifruit, goji berries, lime juice, and cardamom in a large bowl and toss gently but thoroughly.

Stack the mint leaves and cut crosswise into strips about ¼-inch wide. Fluff the strips to separate them. Put half the mint in the bowl and toss gently.

Divide the fruit among four bowls and garnish with the remaining mint. Serve at once.

Per serving: 231 calories, 4 g protein, 1 g fat (0.1 g sat), 57 g carbohydrates, 69 mg sodium, 213 mg calcium, 4 g fiber

FORAGING FOR FLAVOR

Although goji berries have only recently gained popularity in the United States, they have been used as food and medicine in China and Tibet for thousands of years. The most nutritionally dense food in the world, goji berries contain all of the essential amino acids, massive amounts of iron and vitamin C, trace minerals, and antioxidants. In Chinese medicine, they're used as a tonic for the liver, kidney, and immune system. Oh—and they're quite tasty too!

This nutrient-dense dish is luscious and light and will thrill the palate. What's more, the carbohydrates in this breakfast are packed with sense-sharpening and blood-nourishing health benefits.

fruit salad WITH BLUEBERRY-ALMOND CREAM SAUCE

MAKES 4 SERVINGS

1¾ cups **blueberries**

1 cup **coconut cream** from full-fat coconut milk (see sidebar)

4 pitted **medjool dates**

1 tablespoon freshly squeezed **lemon juice**

1 teaspoon **almond extract**

1 cup **strawberries,** halved or quartered lengthwise

1 cup **raspberries**

2 **bananas,** sliced

2 **kiwifruit,** peeled and diced

1 **apple,** diced

Put ¾ cup of the blueberries and the coconut cream, dates, lemon juice, and almond extract in a blender and process until smooth. Transfer to a large bowl, cover, and refrigerate for at least 1 hour or up to 8 hours.

Just before serving, add the remaining cup of blueberries along with the strawberries, raspberries, bananas, kiwifruit, and apple. Toss gently but thoroughly and serve at once.

Per serving: 412 calories, 4 g protein, 18 g fat (15 g sat), 65 g carbohydrates, 38 mg sodium, 71 mg calcium, 10 g fiber

> **COCONUT CREAM:** When a can of full-fat coconut milk is left undisturbed for a long time, the fat rises to the top and hardens. This is called coconut cream. To remove it, be sure not to shake the can. Open the can and carefully scoop out the fat, digging down just until you reach the watery part, which can be reserved for other uses.

gathering flavors . . .

sauces, dips, and condiments

This rich, piquant dip can be served with cut raw vegetables, or it can easily double as a sauce for any number of dishes when thinned with just a little water. Control the heat by increasing or decreasing the amount of chiles. Among anti-inflammatory foods, chiles are rock stars. If you haven't learned to like the heat, now might be a good time to start.

spicy peanut DIP

MAKES 1½ CUPS

1 tablespoon **extra-virgin coconut oil**

2 **shallots**, finely diced

2 tablespoons minced **garlic**

¾ cup roasted **peanuts**

⅓ cup full-fat **coconut milk**

1 tablespoon chopped fresh **red chiles,** or 1 teaspoon **hot red chile powder**

1 tablespoon low-sodium **tamari**

Zest and juice of **1 lime**

Put the oil in a small skillet over high heat. Add the shallots and garlic and stir until the vegetables are soft and slightly caramelized, about 4 minutes. Scrape into a blender and add the peanuts, coconut milk, chiles, tamari, lime zest, and lime juice. Process until the mixture is as thick and smooth as you like, adding a little water if needed to achieve the desired consistency. Scrape into a small bowl and serve.

Per 2 tablespoons: 78 calories, 2 g protein, 6 g fat (3 g sat), 4 g carbohydrates, 118 mg sodium, 7 mg calcium, 1 g fiber

Think of this delightful dip as the paleo version of hummus. It's rich and satisfying but much lighter than its Middle Eastern progenitor. Serve with cut raw vegetables.

roasted pumpkin DIP

MAKES 1½ CUPS

4 cups peeled and diced **pumpkin**

3 tablespoons **extra-virgin olive oil**

¼ teaspoon **sea salt**

1 tablespoon **water**

2 cloves **garlic**, pressed

1 tablespoon freshly squeezed **lemon juice**

¼ cup raw **cashew butter**

Preheat the oven to 400 degrees F.

Put the pumpkin in a medium bowl. Add 2 tablespoons of the oil and the salt and toss until evenly distributed. Line a baking sheet with parchment paper and spread the pumpkin in a single layer. Bake on the center rack for 30 to 40 minutes, until the pumpkin is cooked through and lightly charred. Stir every 10 to 15 minutes to prevent burning. Transfer the pumpkin to a large bowl and sprinkle with the water. Cover and let stand until cool.

Put the pumpkin in a food processor and add the remaining tablespoon of oil and the garlic and lemon juice. Process until smooth, stopping occasionally to scrape down the work bowl. Add the cashew butter and process until well combined. Scrape into a small bowl and serve.

Per 2 tablespoons: 78 calories, 1 g protein, 6 g fat (1 g sat), 2 g carbohydrates, 47 mg sodium, 4 mg calcium, 0 g fiber

A medicinal plant, bitter melon is a powerful blood purifier and tonic that has been used for thousands of years in China to treat a variety of blood disorders. As the name indicates, bitter melon has a strong flavor, which stands up well to the other potent players in this spicy dish.

grilled bitter melon SALSA

MAKES 2 CUPS

3 small **Indian bitter melons**, or 1 large **Chinese bitter melon** (see Foraging for Flavor)

2 **Roma tomatoes**, cut into ½-inch dice

1 ripe but firm **avocado**, cut into ½-inch dice

1 small **white onion**, cut into ¼-inch dice

1 cup coarsely chopped fresh **cilantro**

3 fresh **green serrano chiles**, finely diced

3 tablespoons **flax oil**

2 tablespoons freshly squeezed **lime juice**

½ teaspoon ground **Chimayó chile**

¼ teaspoon **sea salt**

⅛ teaspoon freshly ground **black pepper**

Preheat a charcoal or gas grill on high.

Put the bitter melons on the grill and cook, turning occasionally, until the bitter melons are evenly charred, about 10 minutes. Rinse under cold running water, scraping off as much of the char as possible. Blot dry with a clean dish towel and cut each melon in half lengthwise. Scrape out and discard the seeds with a spoon. Cut the melon halves in half lengthwise again and then crosswise into ¼-inch-thick slices. Transfer to a medium bowl.

Add the tomatoes, avocado, onion, cilantro, chiles, flax oil, lime juice, Chimayó chile, salt, and pepper. Toss with a silicone spatula until well combined. Serve at once.

Per ¼ cup: 97 calories, 1 g protein, 7 g fat (1 g sat), 7 g carbohydrates, 74 mg sodium, 9 mg calcium, 3 g fiber

OPTIONAL CHEAT: Add 1 to 1½ cups of cooked red kidney beans, and eat with fire-heated white corn tortillas.

FORAGING FOR FLAVOR

The best variety of bitter melon is found at Indian markets, where it's known as *karela*. If this food is new to you, be prepared: bitter melon is one of those things you either love or hate. It has a very bitter taste (hence the name), but it does grow on you if you can overcome the initial shock. Once you develop a taste for it, you'll be hooked for life.

This salsa is a delicious dip, and it also works well as a condiment to brighten the palate and stimulate the appetite. But we all know the appetite is already pretty stimulated after a long day of foraging.

pineapple-avocado SALSA

1 cup finely diced **pineapple** (¼-inch pieces)

1 cup finely diced **avocado** (¼-inch pieces)

½ cup finely diced **red onion** (¼-inch pieces)

1 fresh **habanero chile,** finely diced

2 tablespoons freshly squeezed **tangerine juice**

1 tablespoon freshly squeezed **lime juice**

¼ teaspoon **sea salt**

¼ cup coarsely chopped fresh **cilantro or mint** (optional)

Put the pineapple, avocado, onion, chile, tangerine juice, lime juice, and salt in a medium bowl and stir gently but thoroughly with a silicone spatula. Stir in the cilantro, if using. To allow the flavors to meld and develop, let the salsa rest for at least 10 minutes before serving.

Per ¼ cup: 55 calories, 1 g protein, 3 g fat (0.4 g sat), 7 g carbohydrates, 72 mg sodium, 38 mg calcium, 2 g fiber

Edamame are green soybeans that are rich in protein as well as antioxidants. In this arrangement, they come loaded with palate-thrilling flavors thanks to the addition of a classic Japanese condiment. *Shichimi togarashi*, or seven-flavor chile, typically includes black sesame seeds, ground ginger, mandarin orange peel, nori flakes, poppy seeds, *sansho* (prickly ash seeds), *shiso* (perilla leaves), toasted sesame seeds, and—of course—coarsely ground hot red chile powder.

edamame relish WITH AVOCADO AND SHICHIMI TOGARASHI

MAKES 2 CUPS

1 cup frozen **edamame** (see Foraging for Flavor)

1 cup finely diced **avocado** (¼-inch pieces)

3 tablespoons finely diced **shallot** (¼-inch pieces)

3 tablespoons **yuzu juice** or freshly squeezed **lemon juice** (see Foraging for Flavor)

2 teaspoons **toasted sesame oil**

1½ teaspoons **shichimi togarashi** (see Foraging for Flavor)

½ teaspoon **lemon zest**

¼ teaspoon **sea salt**

Fill a small pot about two-thirds full with salted water and bring to a boil over high heat. Add the edamame. When the water returns to a boil, drain the edamame in a strainer and refresh under cold water. Spread on a clean dish towel to dry.

Put the edamame, avocado, shallot, yuzu juice, toasted sesame oil, shichimi togarashi, lemon zest, and sea salt in a medium bowl. Stir gently but thoroughly with a silicone spatula. Serve at once.

Per 2 tablespoons: 38 calories, 2 g protein, 3 g fat (0.4 g sat), 1 g carbohydrates, 40 mg sodium, 9 mg calcium, 1 g fiber

FORAGING FOR FLAVOR

- Edamame is sold frozen in most supermarkets and natural foods stores.

- Look for shichimi togarashi at Japanese or other Asian markets or order from online sources. Although shichimi togarashi provides a distinctive and complex flavor, the relish will still be quite good without it. In a crunch, substitute with ¼ teaspoon of red chile powder or cayenne, ¼ teaspoon of ground ginger, and 1 teaspoon of toasted sesame seeds.

- Yuzu is a Japanese citrus fruit with a unique flavor. The juice and zest are used in a variety of sauces and condiments, including ponzu sauce. Bottled yuzu juice can be found in Asian markets, especially Japanese markets. Although there is no truly similar flavor, freshly squeezed lemon juice is an acceptable substitute for yuzu juice in recipes.

Harissa is the staple hot sauce of Morocco, and there are numerous ways to make it. Some varieties are searingly hot, while others are relatively mild. To control the heat, add a few roasted bell peppers to the mix or remove some of the seeds from the hot red chiles. This version is more nuanced than many—the preserved lemon, mint, and saffron create a secret dance that might go unnoticed at first, but it will slowly appear as if from nowhere once the endorphins kick in. You'll see.

harissa

1 tablespoon **coriander seeds**

1 tablespoon **caraway seeds**

2 **red bell peppers**, roasted and coarsely chopped (see sidebar)

½ pound fresh **hot red chiles**, stemmed and chopped (see variation)

7 cloves **garlic**, coarsely chopped

½ **preserved lemon**, coarsely chopped (optional; see Foraging for Flavor)

1 tablespoon dried **mint**

1 teaspoon **sea salt**

Pinch **saffron** (optional; see Foraging for Flavor)

⅓ cup **extra-virgin olive oil**

Put the coriander and caraway seeds in a small skillet over medium heat. Stir constantly until the seeds release their aroma, about 3 minutes. Don't let them burn! Put the seeds in a mortar and crush into a fine powder. Scrape into a food processor.

Add the roasted bell peppers, chiles, garlic, and optional preserved lemon to the food processor. Pulse until minced. Add the mint, salt, optional saffron, and half the oil and pulse briefly, just until combined.

Scrape into a clean jar and smooth the top. Pour the remaining oil over the top to coat evenly. Cover tightly and store in the refrigerator. After each use, smooth the top and cover with a thin film of oil. Sealed tightly, harissa will keep in the refrigerator indefinitely. But don't put this to the test—enjoy it!

Per 1 tablespoon: 26 calories, 0 g protein, 2 g fat (0.3 g sat), 1 g carbohydrates, 71 mg sodium, 3 mg calcium, 0 g fiber

FORAGING FOR FLAVOR

■ Preserved lemons are a staple of Moroccan and other North African cuisines. They add a tangy, salty flavor to sauces, stews, and other dishes. Look for them in specialty shops and Middle Eastern markets.

■ While a bit on the expensive side, saffron brings incomparable depth of flavor to any dish, and all it takes is a pinch—very little goes a very long way. Over a period of months, a $15 investment in saffron can easily elevate five or six dishes from pedestrian to spectacular.

Learn how to make preserved lemons.

youtu.be/VmRIGqeVBlk

VARIATION: If fresh hot red chiles aren't available, use dried red chiles instead. Simply remove the stems, chop coarsely, put in a medium bowl, and cover with boiling water. After 1 hour, drain and proceed with the recipe.

ROASTED PEPPERS: There's no great secret to making roasted peppers. Even a caveman can do it.

First, preheat the broiler. Then quarter the peppers, removing the seeds and membranes. Put the pieces on a baking sheet, as close together as possible without touching.

Broil the peppers until lightly blackened. Immediately put them into a medium or large bowl and cover tightly. After 10 minutes, pour cold water over the peppers to loosen the skins. Remove and discard the charred skins. Now the roasted peppers are ready to use as directed in any recipe. Store leftover roasted peppers in a tightly sealed container in the refrigerator; they will keep for about 5 days.

Tapenade is a savory favorite named for its essential ingredient, the caper (called *tapeno* in the local dialect of Provence). This flavorful tapenade features green olives and is an excellent appetizer. Or serve it as a snack, a first course, or a condiment with the meal itself.

green olive TAPENADE

MAKES 2 CUPS

½ cup **pine nuts**

1 cup pitted **picholine olives or other green olives** (see Foraging for Flavor)

¾ cup chopped **fresh parsley**

⅓ cup **capers**, rinsed

3 tablespoons **extra-virgin olive oil**

3 cloves **garlic,** pressed

2 teaspoons chopped fresh **thyme**

¼ teaspoon **sea salt**

¼ teaspoon freshly ground **black pepper**

Put the pine nuts in a small bowl and cover with boiling water. Let soak for 1 hour. Drain and rinse the pine nuts well.

Put the pine nuts in a food processor and add the olives, parsley, capers, oil, garlic, thyme, salt, and pepper. Pulse until finely chopped but not smooth. Scrape into a small bowl and serve at room temperature.

Per 2 tablespoons: 56 calories, 1 g protein, 6 g fat (1 g sat), 1 g carbohydrates, 109 mg sodium, 21 mg calcium, 0 g fiber

FORAGING FOR FLAVOR

Picholine olives are preferred in this recipe for their full-bodied, distinctive flavor and firm yet tender flesh. If you would like to try a different green olive, consider the other ingredients in the dish and pick a green olive that will play well with them. It needn't be a French olive; Sicilian Castelvetrano or Greek Halkidiki olives, though very different in character, are two excellent candidates.

CHAPTER FIVE

a fire under every kettle . . .

soups

The distinctive, slightly sour taste of sorrel is brilliant in creamy sauces and soups. You might expect these greens to taste like spinach; however, the overall flavor unexpectedly resembles lemon and is quite mild. In this soup, the sorrel is raw, preserving all its fragile, healthful compounds. A perfect starter for an elegant Stone Age meal.

sorrel SOUP

MAKES 4 SERVINGS

1 cup raw **cashews**

1 tablespoon **extra-virgin olive oil**

2 **shallots,** finely diced

3 cups **water,** plus more as needed

1 cube unsalted **vegetable bouillon**

¼ teaspoon **sea salt**

4 cups **sorrel leaves,** firmly packed (see Foraging for Flavor)

Freshly ground **black pepper**

1 tablespoon snipped fresh **chives,** for garnish

Put the cashews in a medium bowl and cover with boiling water by about 1 inch. Let soak for 1 hour. Drain and rinse the cashews.

Put the oil and shallots in a medium pot over medium heat and cook, stirring frequently, until the shallots are just beginning to sizzle. Spread the shallots in an even layer and decrease the heat to the lowest setting. Cover the pot and let the shallots sweat for 20 minutes. Check occasionally and add 1 tablespoon of water if needed to prevent sticking. Stir in the water, bouillon cube, and salt. Increase the heat to high and bring to a boil.

Put the cashews and sorrel in a blender. Add the shallot mixture and process until smooth. Strain through a sieve into a clean pot and reheat over medium heat until hot, about 5 minutes. Add a light grinding of pepper and stir. Sprinkle with the chives and serve at once.

Per serving: 161 calories, 5 g protein, 11 g fat (2 g sat), 11 g carbohydrates, 208 mg sodium, 74 mg calcium, 4 g fiber

FORAGING FOR FLAVOR

Highly prized in French cuisine, sorrel has a delicious lemony flavor, and tender green leaves that become very soft when cooked. Either puréed or left whole, sorrel is most commonly added to soups and sauces. The leaves can also be added to salads. This is not to be confused with Jamaican sorrel, which is a hibiscus plant, the flowers of which are used to make a refreshing drink.

There are two things about this soup you should know: One, it's very quick and easy to make, and two, you'll be so surprised at how delicious and healthful it is. Keeping the kale raw preserves its nutritional benefits and imparts a bright emerald-green color to the soup. You're going to love this.

green SOUP

1 tablespoon **extra-virgin olive oil**

2 medium **onions**, diced

1 small **napa cabbage**, coarsely chopped

4 cups **water**

2 cubes unsalted **vegetable bouillon**

1 pound frozen **peas**

2 cups coarsely chopped **kale leaves** (center ribs removed before chopping)

Put the oil in a large pot over medium-high heat and add the onions. Cook, stirring frequently, until the onions begin to soften, about 4 minutes. Add the cabbage and stir until the cabbage wilts, about 2 minutes. Stir in the water and bouillon cubes. Increase the heat to high and bring to a boil. Stir in the peas and return to a boil. Decrease the heat to medium and simmer uncovered until the peas are tender but still bright green, about 5 minutes. Remove from the heat and stir in the kale.

Working in batches, process the mixture in a blender until smooth. Strain through a sieve into a clean pot. Reheat and serve.

Per serving: 205 calories, 10 g protein, 6 g fat (2 g sat), 31 g carbohydrates, 234 mg sodium, 167 mg calcium, 9 g fiber

Asparagus is an elegant, unusual plant, rich in vitamin K among other vitamins and minerals. It also is an excellent source of inulin, a naturally occurring prebiotic fiber that is highly beneficial to the flora in the large intestine. Better still, asparagus is delicious!

asparagus-leek SOUP

MAKES 4 SERVINGS

½ cup raw **cashews**

1 pound **asparagus**

2 tablespoons **extra-virgin olive oil**

1 medium **leek,** diced (see sidebar)

2 cups **water**

1 cube unsalted **vegetable bouillon**

1 clove **garlic,** peeled

½ teaspoon **sea salt**

Freshly ground **black or white pepper**

Pinch ground **mace,** for garnish (see
    Foraging for Flavor)

Put the cashews in a small bowl and cover with boiling water by about 1 inch. Let soak for 1 hour. Drain and rinse the cashews.

Wash the asparagus well and snap off any tough ends. Select four attractive asparagus tips and cut them off (each tip should be about 2 inches long). Cut each tip in half lengthwise. Fill a small pot about two-thirds full with salted water and bring to a boil over high heat. Add the asparagus tips. Stir once, then drain in a colander. Refresh under cold running water and lay the tips on a clean dish towel to dry. Cover and set aside. Chop the remaining asparagus coarsely.

Put the oil in a large pot over medium-high heat. Add the leek and cook, stirring constantly, until the leek begins to soften, about 3 minutes. Add the chopped asparagus and cook, stirring frequently, for 2 minutes. Stir in the water, bouillon cube, garlic, and salt. Increase the heat to high and bring to a boil. Decrease the heat to medium and simmer until the vegetables are tender, about 10 minutes. Remove from the heat and let cool slightly.

Put the cashews in a blender. Add the asparagus mixture and process until smooth. Strain through a sieve if desired and return to the pot. Warm over medium-low heat until hot, about 5 minutes. Season with pepper to taste.

Divide the soup among four bowls. Set an asparagus tip cut-side up in the center of each serving, then set another across it, cut-side down. Sprinkle with the mace and serve at once.

Per serving: 149 calories, 4 g protein, 11 g fat (2 g sat), 11 g carbohydrates, 634 mg sodium, 32 mg calcium, 3 g fiber

Mace can be found anywhere spices are sold. It comes from the lacy, deep-red covering that grows around nutmeg seeds; however, mace and nutmeg are remarkably different in both taste and smell. Another difference is that mace is only available ground, but nutmeg is available whole or ground. Nutmeg is much more fragrant when it's freshly grated.

Mace complements asparagus, leeks, and potatoes beautifully and should be used sparingly—a little goes a long way. Inexpensive, mace retains its potency for an extended period if kept tightly covered.

SQUEAKY CLEAN LEEKS: Bits of dirt and grit tend to find their way in between leek leaves, so it's essential to wash this vegetable well before using. Here's the method I use: Keeping the root end intact, cut the leeks in half lengthwise. Rinse thoroughly under cold running water to remove the grit from between the leaves.

Like all squashes, pumpkins are highly nutritious as well as delicious. In this soup, they're joined by a few high-profile flavors, yet they shine through assertively, like the stars in a Paleolithic sky.

curried pumpkin SOUP

MAKES 8 SERVINGS

3 tablespoons **extra-virgin coconut oil**

5 cups diced **onions**

1½ cups diced **green bell peppers**

½ teaspoon **sea salt,** plus more as needed

14 cups peeled and diced **pumpkin**

12 cloves **garlic,** minced or pressed

2 tablespoons **curry powder**

12 cups **water**

3 cubes unsalted **vegetable bouillon**

2 teaspoons lightly crushed **cardamom seeds**

1 cup coarsely chopped fresh **cilantro** leaves and upper stems

Juice of 1 **lemon or lime** (optional)

Put the oil in a large pot over medium-high heat. Add the onions and cook, stirring frequently, until the onions begin to brown, about 10 minutes. Add the bell peppers and salt and stir frequently until the bell peppers begin to soften, about 5 minutes. Add the pumpkin and garlic and cook, stirring frequently, for 2 minutes. Add the curry powder and stir until well combined. Stir in the water and bouillon cubes. Increase the heat to high and bring to a boil. Decrease the heat to medium and simmer uncovered until the vegetables are tender, about 20 minutes. Stir in the cardamom and cilantro and cook for 1 minute longer.

Remove from the heat and stir in the lemon juice, if using. Serve at once.

Per serving: 208 calories, 2 g protein, 6 g fat (6 g sat), 14 g carbohydrates, 242 mg sodium, 25 mg calcium, 1 g fiber

grazing paleo style . . .

salads

Dandelion greens are among the most healthful foods in existence. Like all bitter greens, they act as a powerful blood purifier. When combined with beets as they are here, dandelion greens also help detoxify the liver. In addition, this combo is easy on the palate because the greens' bitter edge is tamed by the beets' sweetness. Brazil nuts bring protein, selenium, and a satisfying crunch to the mix. Health and pleasure!

dandelion salad WITH BEETS

See photo facing page 58

MAKES 4 SERVINGS

1 large bunch very fresh **dandelion greens** (about 6 cups cut leaves)

2 cups grated **beets**

½ cup grated **carrot**

½ cup thinly sliced **red onion**

½ cup thinly sliced **celery heart,** including leaves

⅓ cup freshly squeezed **tangerine juice**

2 tablespoons **white balsamic or champagne vinegar**

2 teaspoons **Dijon mustard**

¼ teaspoon **sea salt**

¼ teaspoon freshly ground **mixed peppercorns** (black, white, green, and pink) **or black only**

¼ cup **walnut oil or extra-virgin olive oil**

½ cup **Brazil nuts,** cut into 4 pieces each

Keeping the dandelion greens in a bunch, hold them by the stems and rinse well under cold running water to remove any grit. Remove any decayed bits, then lay the bunch on a cutting board and cut the leaves and tender stems crosswise at 1-inch intervals. Put in a salad spinner and spin dry, or blot dry with a clean dish towel.

Put the greens in a large bowl and add the beets, carrot, onion, and celery. Toss until well combined.

Put the tangerine juice, vinegar, mustard, salt, and pepper in a medium bowl and whisk until well combined. Add the oil in a thin stream, whisking constantly until emulsified. Pour over the salad and toss thoroughly.

Divide the salad among four plates. Top with the Brazil nuts and serve at once.

Per serving: 383 calories, 7 g protein, 30 g fat (4 g sat), 27 g carbohydrates, 278 mg sodium, 171 mg calcium, 6 g fiber

Sunchokes, also known as Jerusalem artichokes, are related neither to the artichoke nor Jerusalem. In fact, they're the roots of a variety of sunflower plant. This aptly named salad showcases not only the roots but also a few of the sunflower plant's other delights: seeds, sprouted seeds, and seed oil. If you're unable to find a cold-pressed, unrefined sunflower oil as you hunt and gather, use a high-quality extra-virgin olive oil instead.

sunflower SALAD

MAKES 4 SERVINGS

2 tablespoons **sherry vinegar**

2 teaspoons **Dijon mustard**

¼ teaspoon **sea salt**

¼ teaspoon freshly ground **black pepper**

¼ cup unrefined **sunflower oil or extra-virgin olive oil**

6 cups **mixed spring greens**

½ pound **sunchokes,** scrubbed and thinly sliced (see Foraging for Flavor)

2 ripe but firm **avocados,** halved lengthwise and sliced crosswise about ¼-inch thick

2 cups **sunflower sprouts**

⅓ cup raw **sunflower seeds**

To make the dressing, put the vinegar, mustard, salt, and pepper in a medium bowl and whisk to mix well. Add the oil in a thin stream, whisking constantly until emulsified.

Put the greens and sunchokes in a large bowl and toss well. Add the dressing and toss again. Add the avocado slices and toss very gently to avoid breaking them.

Divide the salad among four plates and top with the sunflower sprouts. Sprinkle with the sunflower seeds and serve at once.

Per serving: 376 calories, 6 g protein, 34 g fat (4 g sat), 15 g carbohydrates, 259 mg sodium, 53 mg calcium, 9 g fiber

FORAGING FOR FLAVOR

Sunchokes, also known as Jerusalem artichokes, are the roots of a species of sunflower plant. The tubers look a bit like gingerroot. When cooked, they have a texture similar to a potato, with a far superior flavor.

There were once thousands of varieties of tomatoes, with all kinds of flavors, textures, colors, shapes, and sizes. Heirloom tomatoes are distinctive forms of those original varieties, and it behooves all of us to help retain these gems in the food supply. The best way to do this is to grow, buy, eat, and celebrate heirloom tomatoes at every opportunity. This salad is one way to enjoy their exquisite characteristics.

heirloom tomato salad WITH WATERCRESS

MAKES 4 SERVINGS

1 cup fresh **basil leaves**, firmly packed

½ cup **extra-virgin olive oil**

2 tablespoons aged **balsamic vinegar**

¼ teaspoon **sea salt**, plus more for sprinkling

¼ teaspoon freshly ground **black pepper**

6 cups hydroponically grown **watercress**, leaves only (see Foraging for Flavor)

½ cup thinly sliced **red onion**

3 large **heirloom tomatoes**, sliced about ½-inch thick

Fill a medium saucepan about two-thirds full with water and bring to a boil over high heat. Add the basil and stir once. Drain in a large strainer and immediately rinse under cold running water. Squeeze the basil firmly to express as much water as possible and transfer the leaves to a blender. Add the oil and process until the mixture is smooth and bright green, about 2 minutes, stopping occasionally to scrape down the container. Pour the mixture into a glass and let stand for about 1 hour to allow the solids to settle. Without shaking or stirring, carefully pour the oil through a fine-mesh strainer into a small bowl. Reserve the solids for another use (see Foraging for Flavor).

Put the vinegar, salt, and ⅛ teaspoon of the pepper in a large bowl and whisk until combined. Add 3 tablespoons of the basil oil, whisking constantly until emulsified. Add the watercress and onion and toss thoroughly.

Divide the watercress mixture among four large plates, arranging each portion on one side of the plate. Divide the tomatoes among the plates, slightly overlapping the slices next to the watercress mixture. Drizzle a little of the basil oil over the tomatoes, then sprinkle with the remaining pepper and salt. Serve at once.

Per serving: 281 calories, 3 g protein, 27 g fat (4 g sat), 10 g carbohydrates, 176 mg sodium, 84 mg calcium, 2 g fiber

- When making the basil oil, don't discard the solids. Covered and refrigerated, the solids will keep for about 3 days. Use them up when making soups or other dishes in which the basil flavor will shine.

- You won't need all the basil oil for this recipe, so store the remaining oil for future use. Sealed tightly in a bottle or jar, the remaining basil oil will keep for 1 week in the refrigerator or indefinitely in the freezer. (See sidebar below.)

- Hydroponically grown watercress comes in uniform bunches, each yielding about four cups of leaves with tender upper stems. Another advantage is that no pesticides are needed in hydroponic gardening.

FREEZE OIL FOR LONG-TERM STORAGE: Oil contracts when frozen, so there is no danger of the bottle breaking. To use any type of frozen oil, set the bottle in a bowl of warm water until the oil melts. Pour out the desired amount, then return the bottle to the freezer.

Baby greens of all types present a marvelous opportunity to appreciate everything that's good about plants. These tiny, tender vegetables burst with flavor while providing a variety of healthful phytochemicals. Here, sun-loving greens are perfectly presented, dressed in an earthy mushroom cloak. This salad combines the best the earth has to offer—from both above and below its surface.

baby kale salad WITH BALSAMIC-BRAISED MUSHROOMS

MAKES 4 SERVINGS

3 tablespoons **extra-virgin olive oil**

1 small **red onion,** cut lengthwise into thin slivers

8 ounces large **cremini or button mushrooms,** quartered

¼ cup aged **balsamic vinegar**

½ teaspoon **sea salt**

¼ teaspoon freshly ground **mixed peppercorns** (black, white, green, and pink) **or black only**

1 tablespoon freshly squeezed **lemon juice**

2 teaspoons **Dijon mustard**

2 tablespoons **flax oil or additional extra-virgin olive oil**

8 ounces **baby kale leaves,** course stems removed

Put 1 tablespoon of the olive oil in a large skillet over medium-high heat. Tip the skillet to coat the bottom evenly with the oil and add the onion. Cook, stirring frequently, until the onion begins to soften, about 2 minutes. Add the mushrooms, stir once, and cover tightly. Cook until the mushrooms begin to release their juices, about 2 minutes. Uncover and cook, stirring occasionally, until the juices have been absorbed and the mushrooms are beginning to brown lightly, 2 to 3 minutes. Add 2 tablespoons of the vinegar, ¼ teaspoon of the salt, and ⅛ teaspoon of the pepper and stir until well combined. Decrease the heat to medium-low and continue cooking, stirring frequently, until the liquid thickens slightly, about 3 minutes. Remove from the heat.

While the mushrooms are cooking, prepare the dressing. Put the remaining 2 tablespoons of vinegar and the lemon juice, mustard, and the remaining salt and pepper in a medium bowl. Add the flax oil in a thin stream, whisking constantly until emulsified.

Put the kale in a large bowl. Pour the dressing over the kale and toss until well distributed. Add the mushroom mixture and toss again.

Divide the salad among four plates and serve at once.

Per serving: 233 calories, 5 g protein, 18 g fat (2 g sat), 16 g carbohydrates, 371 mg sodium, 130 mg calcium, 2 g fiber

FORAGING FOR FLAVOR

Consider acquiring a modest amount of the combined black, white, green, and pink peppercorns. The four different peppercorns have unique individual qualities that in combination dazzle the taste buds in a way that black pepper alone cannot. Although this complex flavor isn't suitable for all dishes, it really sparkles in this salad.

Not all people who have a disagreement with Brussels sprouts realize that their argument is really with the cook—the person with poor culinary sense who ruins the delectable sprout by overcooking it. This simple slaw will help the dubious learn to love this fabulously healthful cruciferous vegetable, and in its raw form, no less. However, unless you tell them, guests may not even realize that they're eating Brussels sprouts.

QUICK-AND-EASY brussels sprout slaw

MAKES 4 SERVINGS

1 pound **Brussels sprouts**

1 **fennel bulb,** halved, cored, and sliced

1 **Granny Smith apple,** cut into chunks

3 tablespoons **mellow white miso**

2 tablespoons peeled and grated fresh **ginger**

2 tablespoons **flax oil**

Grated zest of 2 **lemons**

2 tablespoons freshly squeezed **lemon juice**

Remove and discard any dried or discolored outer leaves from the Brussels sprouts and cut off the tough stem ends. Cut the sprouts in half and put them in a food processor. Add the fennel, apple, miso, ginger, oil, lemon zest, and lemon juice. Pulse until chopped, stopping occasionally to scrape down the work bowl. This should take mere seconds.

Divide the salad among four bowls and serve at once.

Per serving: 164 calories, 5 g protein, 7 g fat (1 g sat), 21 g carbohydrates, 325 mg sodium, 81 mg calcium, 6 g fiber

f you've never had mustard greens, this dish will be a special treat—*and* you'll have plenty of homemade blackberry vinegar left over for other adventures! Mustard greens are slightly spicy, with an unusual texture. The ginger in the vinaigrette adds to the exotic effect, as do the mixed peppercorns. The macadamia nuts provide a calming, buttery crunch.

mustard greens WITH GINGER-BLACKBERRY VINAIGRETTE

MAKES 4 SERVINGS

1 cup fresh or frozen **blackberries**

¾ cup **coconut vinegar or white wine vinegar**

1 (2-inch) piece fresh **ginger**, peeled

¼ teaspoon **sea salt**

¼ teaspoon freshly ground **black pepper**

¼ cup **walnut oil**

1 large bunch very fresh **mustard greens** (leaves only; about 12 cups)

1 tablespoon **pink peppercorns**, lightly crushed (optional; see Foraging for Flavor)

1 cup coarsely chopped raw **macadamia nuts**, for garnish

To make the blackberry vinegar, put the blackberries in a medium non-reactive saucepan (such as stainless steel, glass, or enameled cast iron) and crush lightly with a potato masher or silicone spatula. Stir in the vinegar and bring to a simmer over medium heat. Remove from the heat and let cool. Transfer to a blender and process just until the fruit has broken down but the seeds remain mostly whole. Be careful not to blend the seeds or the vinegar will turn bitter. Pour through a strainer into a glass and let settle for a minimum of 20 minutes or preferably 24 hours. Pour through a piece of cheesecloth or a fine-mesh strainer into a jar or bottle, taking care to leave any foam behind. Stored in a tightly sealed jar or bottle, the blackberry vinegar will keep indefinitely.

Slice the ginger as thinly as possible across the grain into coins. Arrange the coins in little stacks on a cutting board. Cut the stacks into thin, tiny matchsticks.

To make the vinaigrette, put ¼ cup of the blackberry vinegar in a medium bowl. Add the ginger, salt, and pepper and whisk until combined. To allow the flavors to develop, let the mixture sit for 10 minutes. Begin whisking again, adding the oil in a thin stream, whisking constantly until emulsified.

Put the mustard greens in a large bowl. Pour the vinaigrette, ginger and all, over the greens. Add the optional peppercorns and toss thoroughly.

Divide the salad among four plates and garnish with the macadamia nuts. Serve at once.

Per serving: 420 calories, 8 g protein, 40 g fat (5 g sat), 16 g carbohydrates, 191 mg sodium, 212 mg calcium, 16 g fiber

FORAGING FOR FLAVOR

Pink peppercorns add an exotic, almost floral note. Like all whole spices, they retain their flavor for years if not ground or crushed. Keep them in a tightly sealed jar until ready to use.

Ripe mangoes are among nature's sexiest fruits—second only to the ripe fig—but green, unripe mangoes have their own special appeal. In Southeast Asia, they're featured in splendid salads and chutneys. If you're new to green mangoes, you may feel unsure when selecting one, but don't fret. You can't go wrong. This salad will prove my point.

green mango SALAD

MAKES 4 SERVINGS

1 large **green mango**

3 cups thinly sliced **napa cabbage**

1 **red bell pepper,** cut into thin strips

8 ounces **mung bean sprouts**

8 **scallions,** thinly sliced on a sharp
   diagonal

¼ cup **mellow white miso**

¼ cup freshly squeezed **lime juice**

1 tablespoon peeled and grated fresh
   ginger

1 fresh **red or green chile,** finely diced

¼ cup **flax oil** (optional)

Grated zest of 2 **limes**

½ cup coarsely chopped fresh **cilantro**

Peel the mango and cut along the pit to free the two halves. Cut away the skin. Cut the mango flesh crosswise into thin slices and put in a large bowl. Add the cabbage, bell pepper, bean sprouts, and scallions and toss thoroughly.

To make the dressing, put the miso, lime juice, ginger, chile, optional oil, and lime zest in a medium bowl. Whisk until well combined.

Pour the dressing over the vegetables and toss until well distributed. Add half the cilantro and toss thoroughly.

Divide the salad among four plates and garnish with the remaining cilantro. Serve at once.

Per serving: 116 calories, 4 g protein, 1 g fat (0 g sat), 24 g carbohydrates, 797 mg sodium, 76 mg calcium, 5 g fiber

Dandelion Salad with Beets, *page 50*

Kale with Peppers, *page 98*

You've probably had artichokes that have been steamed or boiled and served with a side of melted butter for dipping the leaves. However, there are many ways, including raw, to enjoy this vegetable. Here, artichokes are paired with bitter lettuces and sweet fennel. Both are considered digestive aids, so eating this salad as a starter all but guarantees good digestion.

SALAD OF raw artichoke, endive, radicchio, and fennel

MAKES 4 SERVINGS

1 **lemon,** halved

2 cups **water**

2 large **artichokes**

3 tablespoons aged **balsamic vinegar**

1 tablespoon freshly squeezed **lemon juice**

1 tablespoon **Dijon mustard**

½ teaspoon **sea salt**

¼ teaspoon freshly ground **black pepper**

5 tablespoons **extra-virgin olive oil**

3 heads **Belgian endive,** cut lengthwise into strips ¼-inch wide

1 head **radicchio,** halved and cut into strips ¼-inch wide

1 large **fennel bulb,** halved lengthwise, cored, and thinly sliced

½ small **red onion,** cut lengthwise into thin slivers

2 tablespoons chopped fresh **parsley**

Set a fine-mesh strainer above a medium bowl. Squeeze the lemon through the strainer, straining and collecting the lemon juice in the bowl. Reserve the lemon rinds. Stir the water into the lemon juice.

Grasp an artichoke by the stem and snap off the outer leaves until the pale, tender inner leaves are exposed. Cut across the artichoke just above where the leaves are attached. Cut away the darker green tough exterior, exposing the pale inner flesh. Rub all the exposed areas with the juicy side of the lemon rind to prevent discoloration. Using a small spoon, dig out and discard the hairy choke. Cut off the stem. When only the pale artichoke heart remains, slip it into the lemon water. Repeat with the other artichoke.

To make the dressing, put the vinegar, lemon juice, mustard, salt, and pepper in a large bowl and whisk to mix well. Add the oil in a thin stream, whisking constantly until emulsified.

Drain the artichoke hearts and blot dry with a clean dish towel. Slice thinly and add to the dressing. Add the Belgian endive, radicchio, fennel, onion, and 1 tablespoon of the parsley. Toss gently but thoroughly.

Divide the salad among four plates and garnish with the remaining tablespoon of parsley. Serve at once.

Per serving: 309 calories, 8 g protein, 19 g fat (3 g sat), 37 g carbohydrates, 535 mg sodium, 267 mg calcium, 20 g fiber

See how to prepare an artichoke.
youtu.be/bTvhOyDFVmQ

Arugula has a slightly bitter and tangy bite to it, which makes it an interesting partner to grapefruit, and especially a reduction of grapefruit juice, because reducing grapefruit juice tames both the fruit's acidity and bitterness. The roasted hazelnuts provide a bold background note and satisfying crunch.

arugula WITH GRAPEFRUIT REDUCTION AND HAZELNUTS

MAKES 4 SERVINGS

2 cups freshly squeezed **pink grapefruit juice,** strained

4 pitted **medjool dates,** finely diced

1 medium **shallot,** finely diced (about 2 tablespoons)

8 ounces **baby arugula**

¼ teaspoon freshly ground **black pepper**

2 **pink grapefruits,** sectioned

1 cup **hazelnuts,** roasted, peeled, and halved (see sidebar)

Put the grapefruit juice in a small non-reactive saucepan (such as stainless steel, glass, or enameled cast iron). Stir in the dates and shallot and bring to a simmer over medium heat. Cook, stirring occasionally, until the juice has reduced to about ½ cup, about 10 minutes. Remove from the heat and let cool completely.

Put the arugula in a large bowl. Pour the grapefruit juice reduction over the arugula and add the pepper. Toss thoroughly.

Divide the salad among four plates, forming steep mounds. Garnish with the grapefruit sections and hazelnuts. Serve at once.

Per serving: 339 calories, 8 g protein, 17 g fat (1 g sat), 44 g carbohydrates, 11 mg sodium, 158 mg calcium, 6 g fiber

ROASTED AND PEELED HAZELNUTS: Preheat the oven to 350 degrees F. To roast whole hazelnuts, put them on a baking sheet in a single layer and bake for about 7 minutes. If the skins are blistered and the flesh underneath is exposed and lightly browned, remove the nuts from the oven. If not, or if the exposed flesh is only slightly golden, bake for 3 minutes longer and check again.

Immediately remove the nuts from the oven and transfer them onto a clean kitchen towel. Gather the nuts in the center of the towel and fold the sides of the towel over the nuts to encase them snugly. Carefully turn the bundle over so the folded ends of the towel are underneath the nuts. Let the nuts steam in their own heat for about 10 minutes.

Without loosening the towel, knead the bundle firmly for 1 to 2 minutes, rubbing the nuts together inside the towel. This will remove most if not all the skins.

Carefully turn over and open the bundle. Lift out a handful of the nuts at a time, opening your fingers slightly to sift out any skins that may cling. Put the clean nuts in a medium bowl and discard the skins. Repeat with the remaining nuts.

See Alan roasting and peeling hazelnuts.
youtu.be/PZdCSbRqzp8

The success of this salad relies in large part on obtaining very fresh—if possible, garden fresh—and tender Swiss chard leaves. Not that the salad would be terrible with older and less-buttery leaves, but a concerted effort to obtain the most suitable ingredients will always yield a superior dining experience. This salad supplies the evidence: the crunch provided by the red bell peppers and cucumbers is the perfect counterpoint to the yielding yet assertive chard. Trust me.

swiss chard, red pepper, and cucumber SALAD

MAKES 4 SERVINGS

8 large fresh **basil leaves**, torn into small pieces

2 tablespoons **white balsamic vinegar or champagne vinegar**

1 large bunch very fresh **Swiss chard** (about 4 cups cut leaves)

2 **red bell peppers**

4 **baby cucumbers**, sliced about ¼-inch thick

½ **red onion**, thinly sliced

⅓ cup freshly squeezed **tangelo juice**

2 teaspoons **Dijon mustard**

¼ teaspoon **sea salt**

¼ teaspoon freshly ground **black pepper**

¼ cup **walnut oil or extra-virgin olive oil**

Put the basil in a medium bowl. Bruise roughly with the back of a wooden spoon or drink muddler (see Paleo Pointer). Add the vinegar and mash the basil for about 1 minute. Set aside.

Remove the chard's center ribs, stack the leaves, and cut crosswise into strips about ½ inch wide. Quarter the bell peppers lengthwise, remove the seeds and membranes, and cut crosswise into strips about ⅛ inch thick. Put the chard, peppers, cucumbers, and onion in a large bowl. Toss thoroughly until well combined.

To make the dressing, remove the basil from the vinegar and discard the basil. Add the tangelo juice, mustard, salt, and pepper to the vinegar and whisk thoroughly. Add the oil in a thin stream, whisking constantly until emulsified. Pour the dressing over the vegetables and toss thoroughly.

Divide the salad among four plates. Serve at once.

Per serving: 195 calories, 2 g protein, 15 g fat (1 g sat), 8 g carbohydrates, 270 mg sodium, 28 mg calcium, 2 g fiber

PALEO POINTER

A drink muddler is a tool used to bruise fresh ingredients in drinks. Made of hardwood or metal, the operative end is covered with small, spiky points that mash, pierce, and tear fresh ingredients, such as fresh ginger or mint leaves, to release their aromatics.

Aaah. Watercress. Its near-ethereal velvet leaves are irresistible under any circumstances. In the company of fragrant fennel and a sweet-sour apple, however, the peppery and mildly astringent bite of watercress is revelatory. Cider vinegar is widely applauded for its health benefits, but here it's warranted for flavor's sake alone.

watercress, fennel, and apple SALAD

MAKES 4 SERVINGS

2 bunches hydroponically grown **watercress,** leaves and tender upper stems only (see Foraging for Flavor, page 53)

1 **fennel bulb,** halved lengthwise, cored, and thinly sliced

1 small, firm **Winesap or similar apple,** sliced lengthwise into thin wedges

2 tablespoons **cider vinegar**

1 tablespoon **Dijon mustard**

¼ teaspoon **sea salt**

¼ teaspoon freshly ground **mixed peppercorns** (black, white, green, and pink) **or black only**

¼ cup **walnut oil or extra-virgin olive oil**

⅔ cup **walnut halves,** for garnish

Put the watercress, fennel, and apple in a large bowl and toss thoroughly.

To make the dressing, put the vinegar, mustard, salt, and pepper in a medium bowl and whisk until well combined. Add the oil in a thin stream, whisking constantly until emulsified. Pour the dressing over the salad and toss thoroughly.

Divide the salad among four plates and garnish with the walnuts. Serve at once.

Per serving: 294 calories, 5 g protein, 27 g fat (3 g sat), 11 g carbohydrates, 210 mg sodium, 93 mg calcium, 4 g fiber

R adicchio (as the name implies) is an Italian vegetable, but it's always fun to take a food out of its comfort zone and see how well it performs in an unfamiliar environment. Here, transported along with Tuscan kale—another Italian—to the far reaches of Southeast Asia, radicchio takes to its new environment just beautifully.

spicy radicchio and kale SALAD

MAKES 4 SERVINGS

3 tablespoons **mellow white miso**

2 tablespoons **panang or red curry paste**

½ cup full-fat **coconut milk**

¼ cup freshly squeezed **lime juice**

⅓ cup unsalted **crunchy peanut butter**

1 tablespoon finely chopped fresh **red chiles,** or 1 teaspoon **hot red chile powder**

1 head **radicchio,** cored and cut into strips about ¼ inch wide

1 large bunch (about 10 leaves) **Tuscan kale,** center ribs removed, cut into strips about ¼-inch wide

1 **red onion,** cut in half and thinly sliced

2 cups coarsely chopped **fresh cilantro**

To make the dressing, put the miso and curry paste in a large bowl. Mash and stir with a silicone spatula until well combined. Stir in the coconut milk, a little at a time, followed by the lime juice, peanut butter, and chiles. The dressing will be very thick.

Add the radicchio, kale, and onion and stir until the dressing has thinned a little and clings to the vegetables. Stir in the cilantro until evenly distributed.

Divide the salad among four bowls and serve at once.

Per serving: 264 calories, 9 g protein, 16 g fat (7 g sat), 25 g carbohydrates, 692 mg sodium, 130 mg calcium, 5 g fiber

OPTIONAL CHEAT: Stir in 8 ounces of mung bean sprouts when adding the vegetables.

'm always on the hunt for an impromptu masterpiece, and this one came about when a summer afternoon's harvest yielded a combination of ingredients that evoked tabouli, the quintessential Lebanese salad. There wasn't enough parsley to make the genuine dish—and the parsley was of the flat variety, not the traditional curly one—but the other players were virtually calling out for this treatment. The final product is not a true tabouli by any means, but surely its character is "taboulesque."

taboulesque SALAD

MAKES 4 SERVINGS

2 cups coarsely chopped fresh **parsley**

1½ cups **cherry tomatoes,** halved

1 **cucumber,** cut into ½-inch dice

1 **green bell pepper,** cut into ½-inch dice

8 very fresh **scallions,** sliced

2 cloves **garlic,** coarsely chopped

¼ teaspoon **sea salt**

¼ cup freshly squeezed **lemon juice**

¼ cup **extra-virgin olive oil**

¼ cup **flax oil**

Put the parsley, tomatoes, cucumber, bell pepper, and scallions in a large bowl and toss thoroughly.

To make the dressing, put the garlic and salt in a mortar and pound into a mushy paste. Add the lemon juice and stir it into the garlic. Add the olive oil and flax oil, a little at a time, and stir until emulsified. Pour over the salad and toss thoroughly.

Divide the salad among four small bowls or spoon onto lettuce leaves and serve at once.

Per serving: 293 calories, 3 g protein, 27 g fat (3 g sat), 12 g carbohydrates, 168 mg sodium, 86 mg calcium, 3 g fiber

PALEO POINTER

If you don't have a mortar, put the garlic on a cutting board, coarsely chop it, sprinkle it with the salt, and mash it into a paste with the flat side of a knife or the back of a wooden spoon. Scrape the paste into a small bowl and continue with the recipe as directed. Then go straightaway and buy a mortar; it's as paleo as paleo can get.

A slaw is a Northern European affair, not a Mexican one, you may say. And of course, you'd be right. Welcome to the global village, a place unknown to our paleo ancestors.

mexi-SLAW

1 medium **red cabbage**

2 cups grated **carrots**

1 tablespoon coarse **salt**

4 fresh **poblano chiles,** roasted (see sidebar, page 41)

2 small **red onions,** halved lengthwise and thinly sliced

½ cup coarsely chopped fresh **cilantro**

¼ cup **flax oil**

¼ cup freshly squeezed **lime juice**

1 **chipotle chile,** canned or dried and reconstituted in water (optional; see Foraging for Flavor)

2 cloves **garlic,** pressed

1 teaspoon ground **pasilla chile or ancho chile** (see Foraging for Flavor)

½ teaspoon **sea salt**

½ teaspoon **Spanish smoked paprika**

Quarter and core the cabbage, then slice as thinly as possible. Put the cabbage, carrots, and coarse salt in a large bowl and toss well. Let sit for 1 hour to 4 hours. Rinse briefly under cold running water and drain thoroughly in a colander.

Put the cabbage mixture, roasted chiles, onions, and cilantro in a large bowl and toss until well combined.

To make the dressing, put the oil, lime juice, optional chipotle chile, garlic, pasilla chile, salt, and paprika in a blender. Process until smooth and emulsified. Pour over the vegetables and toss thoroughly.

Divide the salad among four small bowls or spoon onto lettuce leaves and serve at once.

Per serving: 244 calories, 6 g protein, 14 g fat (2 g sat), 29 g carbohydrates, 448 mg sodium, 137 mg calcium, 9 g fiber

FORAGING FOR FLAVOR

- Chipotle chiles add much more than heat to a dish. They bring a smoky, potent chile flavor that will simultaneously stand out brightly and blend well with the other ingredients.

- Ground pasilla chile provides an additional layer of genuine Mexican flavor to the dressing. It can usually be found in the Mexican food section of the supermarket. If none is available, however, the salad will still be enjoyable without it.

Aged balsamic vinegar goes so well with so many things, especially young squash. Full disclosure: The vinegar used here is not of the ancient and noble variety, although it still qualifies as "aged." It's but an uppity eighteen-year-old balsamic vinegar that can still work wonders, owing in no small part to the way it is produced. The traditional process concentrates, enriches, and mellows the vinegar until it becomes magical.

baby squash BALSAMICO

MAKES 4 SERVINGS

2 heads **Boston lettuce**

1½ pounds assorted **baby summer squashes**

3 tablespoons aged **balsamic vinegar**

3 tablespoons **extra-virgin olive oil**

1 tablespoon freshly squeezed **lemon juice**

¼ teaspoon **sea salt**

¼ teaspoon freshly ground **black pepper**

1 **red onion,** finely slivered

2 tablespoons chopped fresh **basil**

1 tablespoon thinly sliced fresh **basil leaves,** for garnish

Break up the heads of lettuce, keeping the inner, crisp leaves whole and saving the outer leaves for another use. Wash and spin or pat dry.

Fill a large pot about two-thirds full with salted water and bring to a boil. Add the squashes and cook for 1 minute, stirring frequently, then drain, refresh under cold water, and drain thoroughly. Spread the squashes on a clean dish towel to dry. Cut each squash in half lengthwise.

To make the dressing, put the vinegar, oil, lemon juice, salt, and pepper in a large bowl and whisk until well combined. Stir in the onion and basil. Add the squash and toss gently but thoroughly.

Divide the lettuce among four plates, spreading it out to form beds. Divide the squash mixture among the four beds of lettuce. Drizzle any remaining dressing over the lettuce. Garnish with the basil and serve at once.

Per serving: 170 calories, 6 g protein, 11 g fat (2 g sat), 17 g carbohydrates, 176 mg sodium, 176 mg calcium, 5 g fiber

For paleos who avoid eating grains, tabouli will have gone the way of the bagel. Truth be told, there is very little grain in a genuine tabouli, consisting as it does mainly of coarsely chopped parsley. But one must stick to one's convictions, and a little bulgur is still bulgur. Well, here at last is a vague cousin of tabouli, with cauliflower as a stand-in for the grain. You could steam the cauliflower to more closely approximate bulgur, but left raw it will retain more nutrients, so why not just leave it raw? Your call, of course.

cauliflower TABOULI

MAKES 2 SERVINGS

½ small head **cauliflower**

2 cups coarsely chopped fresh **parsley**

12 **scallions,** coarsely chopped

1 small **tomato,** cut into ¼-inch dice (about ½ cup)

3 tablespoons freshly squeezed **lemon juice**

3 tablespoons **extra-virgin olive oil**

¼ teaspoon **sea salt,** plus more as needed

¼ teaspoon freshly ground **black pepper**

Separate the cauliflower into florets, discarding the thick center stem. Put the florets in a food processor and pulse until finely chopped. The bits should resemble small grains, such as millet or couscous. Measure out ¾ cup of the cauliflower and put in a large bowl, saving the remainder for another use. Stir in the parsley, scallions, and tomato until well combined.

To make the dressing, put the lemon juice, oil, salt, and pepper in a small bowl and whisk. Pour the dressing over the parsley mixture and toss thoroughly.

Divide the salad among four bowls and serve at once.

Per serving: 264 calories, 6 g protein, 21 g fat (3 g sat), 18 g carbohydrates, 369 mg sodium, 118 mg calcium, 7 g fiber

This salad can't accurately be called Lebanese because it combines a traditional Israeli salad with a Lebanese dressing. I hope this flavorful fusion will serve more as a bridge to join the two factions than appear as an affront to either of them. *Shalom! Salaam!* All are welcome!

lebanese-ish SALAD

1½ cups bite-sized pieces **heirloom tomatoes** or halved **cherry tomatoes**

4 **baby cucumbers,** cut into ¼-inch slices

1 **green bell pepper,** cut into ½-inch dice

1 ripe but firm **avocado,** cut into ½-inch dice

1 small **red onion,** halved and thinly sliced

1 cup unsalted cooked or canned **garbanzo beans,** drained and rinsed (optional)

½ cup coarsely chopped fresh **cilantro**

2 cloves **garlic,** coarsely chopped

¼ teaspoon **sea salt**

¼ cup freshly squeezed **lemon juice**

2 tablespoons **extra-virgin olive oil**

⅓ cup **tahini**

Put the tomatoes, cucumbers, bell pepper, avocado, onion, optional garbanzo beans, and half the cilantro in a large bowl and toss thoroughly.

To make the dressing, put the garlic and salt in a mortar (see Paleo Pointer, page 65) and pound into a mushy paste. Add the lemon juice and stir it into the garlic. Stir in the oil, a little at a time, followed by the tahini. If the dressing is very thick, thin with 1 tablespoon of water. Pour over the salad and toss thoroughly.

Divide the salad among four bowls and garnish generously with the remaining cilantro. Serve at once.

Per serving: 228 calories, 4 g protein, 20 g fat (3 g sat), 12 g carbohydrates, 240 mg sodium, 27 mg calcium, 5 g fiber

OPTIONAL CHEAT: While strict paleos avoid legumes, including them up to four times a week is a smart "cheat" for vegans.

Kohlrabi is a largely misunderstood vegetable. It's really no more exotic or unapproachable than its flowering relative, broccoli. Both are highly nutritious, cancer-hostile, and tasty, each in its own way. If you've avoided this odd-looking character until now, here is your chance to try something new.

purple kohlrabi salad WITH WALNUTS

MAKES 4 SERVINGS

2 large **purple or green kohlrabi** with fresh green tops (see Foraging for Flavor)

2 **Granny Smith apples,** cut into matchsticks

3 stalks **celery,** cut into matchsticks

3 tablespoons **white balsamic vinegar or champagne vinegar**

1 tablespoon **Dijon mustard**

¼ teaspoon **sea salt**

¼ teaspoon freshly ground **black pepper**

6 tablespoons **walnut oil**

1 cup **walnut halves**

Separate the kohlrabi from its tentacle-like stems and cut it into matchsticks. Pull the center rib out of the leaves and discard. Stack the leaves and cut into strips similar in dimension to the kohlrabi matchsticks. Put the kohlrabi, greens, apples, and celery in a large bowl and stir until well combined.

To make the dressing, put the vinegar, mustard, salt, and pepper in a medium bowl and whisk until well combined. Add the oil in a thin stream, whisking constantly until emulsified. Pour over the salad and toss thoroughly.

Divide the salad among four plates. Top with the walnuts and serve at once.

Per serving: 446 calories, 6 g protein, 39 g fat (3 g sat), 22 g carbohydrates, 277 mg sodium, 52 mg calcium, 7 g fiber

FORAGING FOR FLAVOR

A member of the wide and diverse family of cruciferous vegetables, kohlrabi has a bulbous root with tentacle-like stems and edible leaves. The root portion is similar in taste and texture to broccoli stems, and is most often peeled before cooking. Small- to medium-sized bulbs are preferable to larger ones, which are often tough.

on't be alarmed by the seeming complexity of this recipe. It comes together very quickly, and you'll be astounded by the intricate flavors that result from so little effort. One word of caution, however: don't try to save leftovers. The cucumbers will release their juices and water down the dressing dreadfully. So eat it all. Take no prisoners!

cucumbers and peppers WITH CHIPOTLE VINAIGRETTE

MAKES 4 SERVINGS

2 **green bell peppers,** roasted and cut into 2-inch squares (see sidebar, page 41)

2 **cucumbers,** quartered lengthwise and sliced about ½ inch thick

1 **red onion,** finely diced

½ cup coarsely chopped fresh **cilantro**

1 dried **chipotle chile,** soaked in warm water to reconstitute

¼ cup freshly squeezed **lime juice**

¼ cup **extra-virgin olive oil**

2 cloves **garlic**

¼ teaspoon **sea salt**

¼ teaspoon freshly ground **black pepper**

Put the roasted peppers, cucumbers, onion, and cilantro in a large bowl and toss until well combined.

To make the dressing, drain the chipotle chile and remove the stem. Put the chile, lime juice, oil, garlic, salt, and pepper in a blender and process until smooth. Pour over the cucumber mixture and toss thoroughly.

Divide the salad among four bowls and serve at once.

Per serving: 178 calories, 2 g protein, 14 g fat (2 g sat), 15 g carbohydrates, 146 mg sodium, 41 mg calcium, 3 g fiber

his salad is a labor of love, to be sure, with several steps and a final assembly that must be executed both quickly and confidently. But rest assured. It's not really difficult, and it's well worth the effort. Guests will swoon with satisfaction and want to linger around your fire all night.

HOT-AND-COLD roasted cauliflower salad

MAKES 4 SERVINGS

1 cup **cashews**

2 tablespoons **currants**

½ cup slivered **almonds**

1 large head **cauliflower**

2 tablespoons **extra-virgin olive oil**

½ teaspoon **sea salt,** plus more as needed

4 **romaine lettuce hearts,** crisp inner leaves only

1 **yellow or white onion,** finely diced

1 cup **water**

1 cube unsalted **vegetable bouillon**

1 teaspoon **ras el hanout or curry powder**

3 tablespoons freshly squeezed **lemon juice**

2 tablespoons chopped fresh **cilantro leaves**

Put the cashews in a medium bowl and cover with boiling water by at least 1 inch. Let soak for 1 hour. Drain and rinse the cashews.

Put the currants in a small bowl and cover with hot water. Let plump for 15 minutes, then drain.

Preheat the oven to 400 degrees F. Spread the almonds on a baking sheet and roast for about 7 minutes, or until lightly browned. Transfer to a small bowl and let cool. Keep the oven on.

Separate the cauliflower into florets. Cut each floret lengthwise into slices about ¼ inch thick. They should look like little tree cross-sections. Coarsely chop any remaining broken or crumbling bits and center stems and set aside.

Line two baking sheets with parchment paper and brush each piece very lightly with 1 teaspoon of the oil. Lay the cauliflower slices on the parchment in a single layer, as close together as possible. Brush the slices very lightly with 2 teaspoons of the oil, then sprinkle with ¼ teaspoon of the salt. Roast for 30 minutes at 400 degrees F, checking during the last 10 minutes to turn any slices that are browning. Turn the slices over and roast for 10 to 15 minutes longer, checking often and removing any that are browned. Put all the roasted slices on an ovenproof plate and set aside. Decrease the oven temperature to 250 degrees F.

Separate the lettuce leaves, cutting off the stem end as needed. Keep the shorter leaves whole and cut the remaining leaves into 4-inch lengths. If any are very wide, cut them in half lengthwise. Put in a large bowl of cold water and soak until ready to serve.

Put the remaining 1 tablespoon of oil in a large saucepan over medium-high heat and add the onion. Cook, stirring frequently, until the onion begins to brown, about 10 minutes. Add the chopped cauliflower pieces and stir until well combined. Cook, stirring frequently, until the mixture is very dry and the cauliflower begins to brown, about 4 minutes. Add the water, bouillon cube, and ras el hanout. Stir until well combined and bring to a boil. Decrease the heat to medium-low, cover, and cook until the vegetables are very tender, about 30 minutes. Transfer to a blender and add about one-third of the roasted cauliflower slices and the cashews. Process until smooth, adding a little water if needed to form a thick cream. Stir in 1 tablespoon of the cilantro. Return to the saucepan and keep warm over low heat.

Put the remaining cauliflower slices in the oven to warm.

Drain the lettuce and spin or towel dry. Put in a large bowl.

To make the dressing, scoop about two-thirds of the cauliflower cream mixture into a medium bowl and stir in the lemon juice. Working quickly, pour the dressing over the lettuce and add about half the warm roasted cauliflower slices. Toss briskly and thoroughly.

Divide the salad among four plates, forming slight mounds. Spoon the remaining warm dressing on top and garnish with the almonds and remaining cauliflower slices and cilantro. Serve at once.

Per serving: 428 calories, 17 g protein, 28 g fat (3 g sat), 40 g carbohydrates, 462 mg sodium, 115 mg calcium, 8 g fiber

T here are many ways to enjoy a jicama, not the least of which is simply sliced and served with lime juice, salt, and ground red chile. This presentation is a little more sophisticated than that, but the soul remains the same.

jicama SALAD

MAKES 4 SERVINGS

1 medium **jicama,** peeled (see Foraging for Flavor)

2 fresh **poblano chiles,** roasted and cut into 2-inch squares (see sidebar, page 41)

1 **red onion,** cut in half and thinly sliced

½ cup coarsely chopped fresh **cilantro**

¼ cup freshly squeezed **lime juice**

¼ cup **extra-virgin olive oil**

1 tablespoon ground **Chimayó chile** (see Foraging for Flavor)

2 cloves **garlic,** minced or pressed

¼ teaspoon **sea salt**

¼ teaspoon freshly ground **black pepper**

Quarter the jicama lengthwise, then cut crosswise into slices about ⅛ inch thick. Put the jicama, roasted poblano chiles, onion, and cilantro in a large bowl and toss until well combined.

To make the dressing, put the lime juice, oil, Chimayó chile, garlic, salt, and pepper in a medium bowl and whisk until emulsified. Pour over the jicama mixture and toss thoroughly.

Divide the salad among four bowls and serve at once.

Per serving: 211 calories, 2 g protein, 14 g fat (2 g sat), 22 g carbohydrates, 152 mg sodium, 37 mg calcium, 9 g fiber

FORAGING FOR FLAVOR

- Native to Mexico, jicama is a tuberous root vegetable. Crisp and very refreshing, jicama contains up to 90 percent water and is rich in vitamins C, B, and A. Jicama is typically a snack food, served with freshly squeezed lime juice and ground chile, but it is also an excellent ingredient in salads.

- If ground Chimayó chile proves difficult to find where you live, select a ground chile that has a lot of flavor but not a lot of heat. You may have to try a few different kinds to familiarize yourself with their attributes, but it's always good to learn more about ingredients that are available to you. You will surely find other uses for them once you get to know them.

Oyster Mushroom and Baby Bok Choy Curry, *page 84*

Artichokes Stuffed with Quinoa, Olives, and Capers, *page 76*

CHAPTER SEVEN

optional cheats for protein . . .

pseudograins

Modern folks know what it's like to scavenge a little, even if that just means searching the cupboards. Still, it's hard to imagine the first person who decided that a giant thistle would be a good thing to eat, but here we are now, and artichokes are absolutely delicious. Stuffed, as in this dish, they also make for an impressive presentation.

artichokes STUFFED WITH QUINOA, OLIVES, AND CAPERS

See photo facing previous page

MAKES 4 SERVINGS

¾ cup **quinoa**

1¼ cups **water**

2¼ teaspoons **sea salt**

1 cube unsalted **vegetable bouillon** (optional; see Foraging for Flavor)

4 large **artichokes**

2 **lemons**

1 **bay leaf**

2 tablespoons **extra-virgin olive oil**

1 small **red onion,** diced

1 clove **garlic,** minced

12 **green olives,** preferably Castelvetrano, pitted and coarsely chopped (see Foraging for Flavor)

2 tablespoons **capers**

Freshly ground **black pepper**

2 tablespoons coarsely chopped **parsley**

See how to prepare an artichoke.
youtu.be/bTvhOyDFVmQ

Rinse the quinoa and put it in a small saucepan. Add the water, ¼ teaspoon of the salt, and the optional bouillon cube. Bring to a boil over high heat. Decrease the heat to low, cover, and cook for 15 minutes. Remove from the heat. Fluff the grains with a silicone spatula and replace the cover.

While the quinoa is cooking, prepare the artichokes. Grate the zest from the lemons onto a small plate. Cover the zest and set it aside. Juice one of the lemons through a strainer into a medium saucepan and save the rinds. Add the remaining 2 teaspoons of salt, the bay leaf, and enough water to fill the saucepan a little more than halfway.

Grasp an artichoke by the stem and snap off the outer leaves until the pale, tender inner leaves are exposed. Cut across the artichoke just above where the leaves are attached. Cut away the tough, darker-green exterior of the artichoke, exposing the pale inner flesh. Rub all the exposed areas with the juicy side of the lemon rind, to prevent discoloration. Using a small spoon, dig out and discard the hairy choke. Cut off the stem. If the stem is 1 inch or more in diameter, carve away the green, fibrous exterior to expose the pale, tender heart. Dice the inner stem, toss with a little lemon juice, and set aside. Drop the prepared artichoke into the saucepan containing the lemon water. Repeat with the remaining artichokes.

Put the saucepan over high heat and bring to a boil. Decrease the heat to medium, cover, and simmer until the artichokes are just tender, about 8 minutes. The tip of a knife should penetrate and slip back out easily. Remove the artichokes with a slotted spoon and invert them on a plate to drain.

Preheat the oven to 350 degrees F.

Put the oil in a large saucepan over high heat and add the onion. Cook, stirring frequently, for about 2 minutes. Decrease the heat to medium and add the garlic and diced artichoke stems, if using. Cook, stirring frequently, until the vegetables are soft, about 10 minutes. Add the olives and capers and stir until warmed through, about 2 minutes. Season with pepper to taste. Remove from the heat and stir in the quinoa and parsley.

Turn the artichokes over and divide the quinoa mixture among them, forming mounds. Press gently to compact the mounds. Put the stuffed artichokes on a baking sheet and bake on the middle rack for about 15 minutes, until hot. Serve at once.

Per serving: 264 calories, 12 g protein, 13 g fat (1 g sat), 41 g carbohydrates, 612 mg sodium, 126 mg calcium, 13 g fiber

FORAGING FOR FLAVOR

- Although vegetable bouillon cubes are optional, they do fortify the flavor of many other ingredients, especially grains—or in paleo applications, pseudograins.

- Castelvetrano olives are bright green Sicilian olives with a very fresh taste. If you have any trouble finding them, by all means use whichever green olives taste good to you.

This savory dish combines a wild seed from the Andes (quinoa), a European allium vegetable (leeks), and a rare fungus from northern Italy (in the form of white truffle oil). This is a combination our paleo ancestors couldn't have imagined. Ours is an exciting time in which to be alive!

quinoa WITH LEEKS AND WHITE TRUFFLE OIL

MAKES 4 SERVINGS

1 cup **quinoa**

1½ cups **water**

1 cube unsalted **vegetable bouillon**

½ teaspoon **sea salt**

4 **leeks** (see sidebar, page 47)

2 tablespoons **extra-virgin olive oil**

Freshly ground **black pepper**

2 teaspoons **white truffle oil** (see Foraging for Flavor)

2 tablespoons snipped fresh **chives**

Rinse the quinoa and put it in a small saucepan. Add the water, bouillon cube, and ¼ teaspoon of the salt. Bring to a boil over high heat. Decrease the heat to low, cover, and cook for 15 minutes. Remove from the heat. Fluff the grains with a silicone spatula and replace the cover.

While the quinoa is cooking, prepare the leeks. Cut the leeks in half lengthwise before washing. Cut off the root ends, then cut the leeks in half lengthwise again. Cut them crosswise at ½-inch intervals.

Put the oil in a large saucepan over medium-high heat and add the leeks. Stir until the leeks are coated with the oil. Add the remaining ¼ teaspoon of salt and cook, stirring frequently, until the leeks are tender, about 10 minutes. Add the quinoa and stir until well combined. Season with pepper to taste and heat, stirring almost constantly, until the quinoa is warmed through, 3 to 4 minutes. Stir in the truffle oil and half the chives.

Divide among four plates, garnish with the remaining chives, and serve at once.

Per serving: 278 calories, 11 g protein, 16 g fat (2 g sat), 44 g carbohydrates, 354 mg sodium, 133 mg calcium, 10 g fiber

FORAGING FOR FLAVOR

White truffle oil is available in small bottles at specialty stores. It may strike you as expensive at first, but when you consider that you'll never use more than a few teaspoons in a single dish, the price will seem much more reasonable. To learn how to preserve the oil indefinitely in the freezer, see the sidebar on page 53. If you can't find white truffle oil, just call this dish Quinoa with Leeks and soldier on; it will still be good without the sublime truffle oil.

Quinoa makes a delicious whole-food stand-in for couscous, the staple food of Morocco. The two are in fact quite different, but their similarities suffice for most applications, and the health benefits of quinoa make it a superior choice over any refined carbohydrate—even the wonderful couscous. This, of course, is not meant to be an authentic Moroccan dish, but the flavors and overall effect are reminiscent of that superlative cuisine.

quinoa WITH GARNET YAMS AND MOROCCAN SPICES

MAKES 4 SERVINGS

1 cup **quinoa**

1½ cups **water**

2 cubes unsalted **vegetable bouillon**

½ teaspoon **sea salt**

2 teaspoons **extra-virgin coconut oil**

4 very thin **garnet yams**, peeled and cut into 1-inch lengths

2 teaspoons **ras el hanout or curry powder,** plus more as needed

¼ teaspoon ground **cinnamon**

8 **scallions,** thinly sliced

1 cup coarsely chopped fresh **cilantro**

Rinse the quinoa and put it in a small saucepan. Add the water, one of the bouillon cubes, and ¼ teaspoon of the salt. Bring to a boil over high heat. Decrease the heat to low, cover, and cook for 15 minutes. Remove from the heat. Fluff the grains with a silicone spatula and replace the cover.

While the quinoa is cooking, prepare the yams. Select a skillet wide enough to accommodate all the yams in one layer. Coat the skillet with the oil and put the yams cut-side down in the pan so they stand upright like cylinders. Carefully pour in enough water to come about ½ inch up the sides of the yams. Break the remaining bouillon cube into a few small pieces and drop them into the water. Dust the tops of the yams with the ras el hanout and the remaining ¼ teaspoon of salt.

Put the skillet over medium-high heat and bring to a simmer. Decrease the heat to medium, cover, and simmer until the yams are tender, about 10 minutes. Remove the cover and cook until no water remains in the skillet and the yams caramelize lightly on the bottom, 10 to 15 minutes. Lift and shake the pan to caramelize the sides of the yams just a bit. Add the quinoa and cinnamon, gently stir until well combined, and heat until warmed through, about 5 minutes. Gently stir in the scallions and cilantro. Taste and add more ras el hanout if desired. Serve at once.

Per serving: 274 calories, 12 g protein, 9 g fat (3 g sat), 56 g carbohydrates, 272 mg sodium, 100 mg calcium, 13 g fiber

Everyone who cooks—or even tries to cook—has at one time or another had to face a refrigerator jammed with a disparate array of less-than-fresh, use-it-or-lose-it vegetables. I imagine our paleo ancestors also devised unique ways to combine the finds of the day (or yesterday). Turns out that's the perfect opportunity to pull off something as weird and wonderful as this dish right here.

ODDS AND ENDS wild rice pilaf

MAKES 4 SERVINGS

½ cup **wild rice**, rinsed (see Foraging for Flavor)

1½ cups **water**

1 cube unsalted **vegetable bouillon**

½ teaspoon **sea salt**

2 tablespoons **extra-virgin olive oil**

3 cups diced **onions**

2 cups diced **mushrooms**

1 cup diced **celery**

1 cup diced **beet** (see Foraging for Flavor)

¾ cup peeled and diced **broccoli stems**

¾ cup diced **carrot**

¾ cup sliced **baby zucchini**

3 cups coarsely chopped **kale** (whatever kind you have)

2 tablespoons **fines herbes**

¼ teaspoon freshly ground **black pepper**

8 **scallions,** thinly sliced

2 tablespoons chopped fresh **parsley**

Put the wild rice, water, bouillon cube, and ¼ teaspoon of the salt in a small saucepan and bring to a boil over high heat. Decrease the heat to medium, cover, and simmer for 25 minutes. If some water remains in the bottom of the pan, continue cooking until it has been absorbed. Remove from the heat and set aside.

Put the oil in a large saucepan over medium-high heat and add the onions. Cook, stirring frequently, until the onions begin to soften, about 4 minutes. Add the mushrooms, celery, beet, broccoli stems, and carrot and stir until well combined. Cook, stirring frequently, for 10 minutes. Add the zucchini, kale, fines herbes, and remaining ¼ teaspoon salt and stir until well combined. Decrease the heat to medium and cook, stirring occasionally, until the vegetables are tender, about 10 minutes longer.

Add the pepper and the wild rice and heat, stirring almost constantly, until warmed through, 3 to 4 minutes. Stir in half the scallions and parsley.

Divide among four plates and garnish with the remaining scallions and parsley. Serve at once.

Per serving: 296 calories, 10 g protein, 10 g fat (2 g sat), 48 g carbohydrates, 429 mg sodium, 157 mg calcium, 9 g fiber

- True wild rice, which comes from Minnesota and is gathered by Native Americans by canoe, has an entirely different flavor and texture from cultivated "wild" rice and cooks much faster. If you prefer the less expensive—and easier to find—cultivated version, you'll need to increase the water to 3 cups and the cooking time to 1 hour. Wild rice is done when the grains split apart and become tender-chewy.

- If you're up for a hunt, scout around for a Chioggia beet for this recipe. Chioggia beets are an heirloom variety, sometimes called Candy Cane beets or Bullseye beets because they have a lovely striped red-and-white interior. A Chioggia beet won't color the entire dish the way a standard purple beet will.

on't let the recipe title scare you off. There is very little real resemblance between what is offered here and the greasy fast-food version made with white rice. Really, paleos would approve this cheat: this is a dish to build healthy cells, not bulging bellies. The taste, however, is indulgent; if you've ever had a truly well-executed fried rice, this one will bring back fond memories.

PINEAPPLE fried rice

MAKES 4 SERVINGS

¾ cup **wild rice,** rinsed (see Foraging for Flavor, page 81)

1½ cups **water**

1 cube unsalted **vegetable bouillon**

¼ teaspoon **sea salt**

2 cups diced **pineapple** (½-inch pieces)

1¼ cups coarsely chopped fresh **cilantro**

2 fresh **red chiles,** thinly sliced

8 **scallions,** sliced

2 tablespoons **extra-virgin coconut oil**

1½ cups thinly sliced **shallots**

2 tablespoons low-sodium **tamari**

½ cup toasted slivered **almonds** for garnish

Put the wild rice, water, bouillon cube, and salt in a small saucepan and bring to a boil over high heat. Decrease the heat to medium, cover, and simmer for 25 minutes. If some water remains in the pan, continue cooking until it has been absorbed. Remove from the heat and set aside.

Combine the pineapple, 1 cup of the cilantro, and the chiles and scallions in a medium bowl.

Put the oil in a large saucepan over medium-high heat and add the shallots. Cook, stirring frequently, until the shallots begin to brown, about 5 minutes. Add the wild rice and heat, stirring almost constantly, until warmed through, 2 to 3 minutes. Add the pineapple mixture and tamari and heat, stirring gently, until warmed through, 3 to 5 minutes. Serve at once, garnished with the almonds and remaining ¼ cup of cilantro.

Per serving: 463 calories, 13 g protein, 24 g fat (8 g sat), 55 g carbohydrates, 556 mg sodium, 104 mg calcium, 4 g fiber

Use only 100 percent buckwheat soba noodles when making these cakes. Feel free to use leftover noodles, or make the cakes using freshly cooked soba—why not? The combination of hot, crispy soba cakes and cool, creamy avocado is stunningly delectable.

buckwheat soba cakes WITH AVOCADO

MAKES 4 SERVINGS

8 ounces **buckwheat soba noodles** (see Foraging for Flavor)

2 teaspoons **toasted sesame oil**

8 **scallions,** thinly sliced on a sharp diagonal

¼ cup **sesame seeds**

2 tablespoons **extra-virgin coconut oil**

2 ripe **avocados,** sliced ¼-inch thick

Fill a large pot about two-thirds full with water and bring to a boil over high heat. Add the noodles, stirring to prevent sticking. Cook, stirring occasionally, until the noodles are just tender, about 5 minutes. Drain in a colander and rinse with cold water. Drain thoroughly and put in a medium bowl. Add the toasted sesame oil and toss well to coat.

Set aside about ¼ cup of the scallions and 1 tablespoon of the sesame seeds. Add the remaining scallions and sesame seeds to the noodles and toss until the noodles are well coated. Divide the noodles into four equal portions.

Put the coconut oil in a large skillet over medium-high heat. Add the four separate portions of noodles and flatten them into cakes with a spatula. Cook until the bottoms are crispy, 3 to 4 minutes. Turn the cakes over and cook on the other side until crispy, 3 to 4 minutes. Don't let them burn!

Put one soba cake on each of four plates. Arrange the avocados over the cakes in a decorative pattern. Garnish with the reserved scallions and sesame seeds and serve at once.

Per serving: 507 calories, 10 g protein, 29 g fat (10 g sat), 56 g carbohydrates, 18 mg sodium, 139 mg calcium, 12 g fiber

FORAGING FOR FLAVOR

Although traditional soba noodles made with 100 percent buckwheat and no wheat can be difficult to find, they're worth hunting for. Online purveyors of macrobiotic foods offer several varieties, including some that feature such ingredients as lotus root, wild yam, or mugwort.

The secret to this earthy dish is not to overcook the buckwheat or the kale so that each stands up to the other, providing a satisfying bite. The Aleppo pepper is optional; the result will still be quite gratifying with a little less heat.

kasha WITH KALE

MAKES 4 SERVINGS

1½ cups **buckwheat groats**

1 teaspoon **sea salt**

1 tablespoon **extra-virgin olive oil**

3 cups diced **onions**

4 cloves **garlic,** minced

2 teaspoons crushed **Aleppo pepper,** or ½ teaspoon **cayenne** (optional; see Foraging for Flavor)

¼ teaspoon freshly ground **black pepper**

8 cups coarsely chopped **kale leaves,** firmly packed (about 2 large bunches)

Zest and juice of 1 **lemon**

⅓ cup raw or toasted **pumpkin seeds**

Fill a large pot about two-thirds full with water and bring to a boil over high heat. Add the buckwheat and ¾ teaspoon of the salt, stirring well. Return to a boil. Decrease the heat to medium and simmer until tender, about 12 minutes. Drain and set aside.

Put the oil in a large saucepan over medium-high heat and add the onion. Cook, stirring frequently, until the onions soften and just begin to brown at the edges, about 5 minutes. Add the garlic, optional Aleppo pepper, and black pepper, and cook, stirring constantly, until the garlic begins to color lightly, about 1 minute. Add the kale and stir until well combined. Cook, stirring frequently, until the kale wilts, about 2 minutes. Add the remaining ¼ teaspoon of salt and cook, stirring frequently, until the kale is tender, 5 to 7 minutes. Add a small amount of water, about 1 tablespoon at a time, as needed to keep the mixture moist. When the kale is tender, add the buckwheat, stirring until well combined. Cook, stirring almost constantly, until warmed through, 3 to 5 minutes. Remove from the heat and stir in the pumpkin seeds, lemon zest, and lemon juice until well combined. Serve at once.

Per serving: 431 calories, 23 g protein, 11 g fat (1 g sat), 74 g carbohydrates, 70 mg sodium, 230 mg calcium, 14 g fiber

FORAGING FOR FLAVOR

Aleppo pepper is optional here, but including it will add both the dimension of heat and its own distinctive flavor, a sweet-sour note reminiscent of sun-dried tomatoes.

CHAPTER EIGHT

more optional cheats for protein . . .

legumes

Black-eyed peas are truly exceptional in and of themselves, but given the right venue, they shine like rock stars. "Étouffé" means "smothered," and these black-eyed peas are truly smothered in a rich blanket of flavor. This is a dish that takes a little effort, but the results are well worth the trouble. It's also one that you might as well make plenty of, because it doesn't take that much more out of you to make twice the quantity.

black-eyed peas ÉTOUFFÉS

MAKES 8 SERVINGS

2 tablespoons **extra-virgin olive oil**

4 cups diced **red onions**

2 cups diced **celery**

2 **red bell peppers**, roasted, peeled, and diced (see sidebar, page 41)

2 **yellow bell peppers**, roasted, peeled, and diced (see sidebar, page 41)

2 **orange bell peppers**, roasted, peeled, and diced (see sidebar, page 41)

3 tablespoons minced **garlic**

2 fresh **green serrano chiles**, diced

2 fresh **red serrano chiles** or additional **green chiles**, diced

1 teaspoon **sea salt**

2 teaspoons **Spanish smoked paprika**

5 cups unsalted cooked or canned **black-eyed peas**, with liquid

1 cup chopped **fresh parsley**

8 **scallions**, very thinly sliced

1 cup **flax oil** (optional)

1 tablespoon crushed **Aleppo pepper**, or 1 teaspoon **cayenne**

Put the oil in a large saucepan over medium-high heat. Add the onions and cook, stirring frequently, until the onions have softened and are just beginning to color lightly, about 4 minutes. Add the celery and stir until well combined. Cook, stirring frequently, until the vegetables are nearly dry, about 10 minutes. Add the roasted bell peppers, garlic, chiles, salt, and paprika and stir until well combined. Cover and decrease the heat to medium-low. Cook, stirring frequently, for 30 minutes. If necessary, add the black-eyed pea cooking liquid or plain water, 1 tablespoon at a time, to prevent sticking.

When the vegetables are tender and a sauce has formed, add the black-eyed peas. Warm through, stirring constantly, over medium-high heat. Remove from the heat and stir in half the parsley.

Serve in bowls, garnished with a mound of the scallions and the remaining parsley in the center, rimmed by a thin moat of the optional flax oil, and generously dusted with the Aleppo pepper. Invite guests to stir everything together just before eating.

Per serving: 219 calories, 5 g protein, 5 g fat (1 g sat), 55 g carbohydrates, 318 mg sodium, 171 mg calcium, 8 g fiber

I n Egypt, fava beans, known there as *ful*, are cooked at a low temperature for a long time—overnight, traditionally—resulting in a firm yet creamy bean with incomparable flavor. However, excellent results can be still achieved by taking a modern shortcut. Canned fava beans work quite well in this dish, as you will see.

fennel and fava beans WITH LEMON

MAKES 4 SERVINGS

4 tablespoons **extra-virgin olive oil**

2 **fennel bulbs**, diced (about 4 cups)

1 can (15 ounces) unsalted **fava beans,** drained and rinsed (see Foraging for Flavor)

½ teaspoon **sea salt**

3 tablespoons freshly squeezed **lemon juice**

2 tablespoons chopped fresh **parsley**

Finely grated zest of 1 **lemon,** for garnish

Put 1 tablespoon of the oil in a medium saucepan over medium-high heat. Add the fennel and cook, stirring frequently, until it has softened and is just beginning to brown, about 10 minutes. Stir in the fava beans and salt and warm through, 5 to 10 minutes. Remove from the heat and stir in the remaining 3 tablespoons of oil and the lemon juice and half the parsley. Stir gently until well combined.

Divide among four small bowls. Garnish with the remaining parsley and the lemon zest. Serve at once.

Per serving: 255 calories, 9 g protein, 14 g fat (2 g sat), 25 g carbohydrates, 597 mg sodium, 87 mg calcium, 9 g fiber

FORAGING FOR FLAVOR

Although fava beans may seem exotic, they can be found at most natural food stores as well as Middle Eastern markets.

The combination of beans or lentils with greens is common in the Middle East and Africa (where humans are thought to have originated), and it's a delicious one. In this version, the beans are distinctly Mexican and the chard is European, a combination that essentially joins four continents—and delectably so. How wonderful that food creates a bridge to other cultures, both present and past.

black beans WITH RED CHARD

MAKES 4 SERVINGS

1 large bunch **red Swiss chard** (about 8 stalks)

2 tablespoons **extra-virgin olive oil**

1 **red onion,** diced

4 cloves **garlic,** minced

2 cups unsalted cooked or canned **black beans,** with liquid

1 tablespoon ground **pasilla chile** (optional; see Foraging for Flavor)

1 tablespoon **chipotle chile purée** (see sidebar)

1 teaspoon **Spanish smoked paprika**

½ teaspoon **sea salt,** plus more as needed

Remove the chard's center ribs. Dice the ribs and set on a plate. Chop the leaves coarsely.

Put the oil in a large saucepan over medium-high heat. Add the onion and cook, stirring frequently, until it has softened and is just beginning to color lightly. Add the chard stems and garlic and cook, stirring frequently, until the vegetables are glistening and fragrant, about 3 minutes. Add the chard leaves and stir until wilted, about 1 minute. Add 1 cup of the bean cooking liquid or plain water and the pasilla chile, chipotle purée, paprika, and salt and stir until well combined. Bring to a boil, decrease the heat to medium, and simmer, stirring frequently, until the vegetables are tender, about 15 minutes.

Stir in the black beans and warm through. Taste and add more salt if desired. Serve at once.

Per serving: 221 calories, 10 g protein, 8 g fat (1 g sat), 30 g carbohydrates, 523 mg sodium, 80 mg calcium, 10 g fiber

FORAGING FOR FLAVOR

Pasilla is a very distinctive chile, and black beans benefit tremendously from the addition of even a small amount. The name "pasilla" is related to the Spanish *pasa* or English "raisin," partly because the whole pasilla chile looks a bit like a long raisin, but also because it has a slightly sweet undertone enfolded in its spicy, smoky leading flavor. If you're not able to find ground pasilla chile at a local market, consider ordering it from an online source. Tightly sealed, it will remain potent for years, and you'll be glad to have it for numerous uses.

CHIPOTLE CHILE PURÉE: To make the chipotle chile purée, empty one or more cans of chipotle chiles into a blender and process until smooth. Scrape into a clean glass jar, seal tightly, and store in the refrigerator indefinitely.

At first glance, you may think the extensive use of onion and its allium relatives gratuitous in this recipe. However, when you take your first bite of the finished dish, you'll understand right away why it's done this way and why the recipe has been formulated to yield such a large quantity. The leftovers are just as enjoyable, even three days running. Lentils never had it this good.

ALLIUM-RICH lentils

3 cups **French green lentils**

¼ cup **extra-virgin olive oil**

1 large **onion**, diced

2 large **shallots**, diced

4 **leeks**, diced (see sidebar, page 47)

32 **scallions**, sliced

3 tablespoons minced **garlic**

2 cups diced **carrots**

3 stalks **celery**, diced

9 cups **water**

3 cubes unsalted **vegetable bouillon**

1 teaspoon **sea salt**

3 **bay leaves**

Pick over the lentils to remove any stones or other debris. Wash and drain the lentils thoroughly.

Put the oil in a large saucepan over medium-high heat. Add the onion and cook, stirring frequently, until they have softened and are just beginning to color lightly, about 5 minutes. Add the shallots and cook, stirring frequently, until they soften, about 4 minutes. Add the leeks, scallions, and garlic and cook, stirring frequently, for 4 minutes. Add the carrots and celery and stir until well combined. Cook, stirring frequently, for 10 minutes. Add the lentils and stir until well combined. Add the water, bouillon cubes, salt, and bay leaves and bring to a boil. Decrease the heat to medium and simmer until the lentils are tender, about 1 hour. If you need to add water to keep the lentils from drying out, use boiling water. Serve hot.

Per serving: 382 calories, 16 g protein, 7 g fat (1.5 g sat), 45 g carbohydrates, 353 mg sodium, 128 mg calcium, 9 g fiber

Spoiler alert: this is a showstopper, both in appearance and flavor. There is a slight trick to making it, because the tempeh needs to be hot and crunchy while the rest of the dish is cool and soft, but you'll master this very quickly. Invite friends. Get out your camera.

avocado and tempeh towers WITH SPICY RED PEPPER SAUCE

MAKES 4 SERVINGS

4 **red bell peppers**, roasted (see sidebar, page 41)

1 tablespoon crushed **Aleppo pepper**, or 1 teaspoon **cayenne**

2 cloves **garlic**

½ teaspoon **sea salt**

3 tablespoons **flax oil**

2 ripe but firm **avocados**, cut into ½-inch dice

8 **scallions**, thinly sliced

2 fresh **hot green chiles**, finely diced

2 tablespoons freshly squeezed **lemon juice**

¾ cup **extra-virgin coconut oil**

8 ounces **tempeh**, cut into ½-inch cubes (see Foraging for Flavor)

2 tablespoons chopped fresh **parsley**, for garnish

To make the spicy red pepper sauce, put three of the roasted bell peppers in a blender and add the Aleppo pepper, garlic, and ¼ teaspoon of the salt. Process until smooth. With the blender running, add the flax oil. Pour into a small pitcher or squeeze bottle and set aside.

To make the towers, cut the remaining roasted bell pepper into ½-inch dice and put in a medium bowl. Add the avocados, scallions, chiles, lemon juice, and the remaining ¼ teaspoon of salt. Toss gently to avoid mashing the avocado.

Preheat the oven to 300 degrees F. Put a folded paper towel on a plate.

Put the coconut oil in a small skillet over high heat. As soon as the oil is hot (375 degrees F on a thermometer), carefully add half the tempeh. Stir gently to keep the cubes moving and cook until the tempeh is lightly browned. Remove with a slotted spoon and set on the paper towel to drain. Transfer the tempeh to a baking sheet and put in the oven to keep warm. Repeat with the remaining tempeh.

Put a ring mold (see Paleo Pointer), 2 inches in diameter and 4 inches tall, in the center of a salad plate. Remove the tempeh from the oven and add to the avocado mixture. Working quickly, fold the tempeh into the mixture. Pack the mold firmly with one-quarter of the mixture, smoothing the top. Lift the mold up to release the mixture and create a tower. Repeat with the remaining mixture to create four towers on four separate salad plates. Surround the towers with the spicy red pepper sauce. Garnish with the parsley and serve at once.

Per serving: 352 calories, 15 g protein, 28 g fat (5 g sat), 21 g carbohydrates, 526 mg sodium, 258 mg calcium, 9 g fiber
NOTE: Analysis doesn't include oil for frying.

FORAGING FOR FLAVOR

Tempeh is a fermented soybean cake and is very high in protein. It comes packaged, usually about 3 inches wide, 5 inches long, and ¾ inches thick. Look for it in natural food stores, in the refrigerated section.

PALEO POINTER

A ring mold, available at most kitchen supply stores, is a simple stainless steel band, open at both ends, that allows the cook to form food into a particular shape for aesthetic plating. Ring molds come in various dimensions and shapes; some are square, triangular, or hexagonal. If you don't have a ring mold like the one described, don't be deterred. You can use anything that resembles a ring mold, such as a biscuit cutter or a can with both ends removed. If no device is available, simply form an attractive mound in the center of the plate. That's what our paleo ancestors would have done.

f rom few ingredients, a full-flavored dish emerges. And quickly! This could easily become your favorite go-to tofu recipe.

spicy fragrant tofu WITH PEANUTS

MAKES 4 SERVINGS

3 stalks **lemongrass** (see Foraging for Flavor)

¼ cup low-sodium **tamari**

3 cloves **garlic**, minced or pressed

2 fresh **red Thai or serrano chiles**, finely diced

1 teaspoon ground **turmeric**

1 teaspoon **palm sugar** (optional)

12 ounces **firm tofu**, sliced 1-inch thick

2 tablespoons **extra-virgin coconut oil**

¼ cup roasted **peanuts**, coarsely chopped

1 cup whole fresh **basil leaves**, firmly packed

Remove the root end and the tough, dry outer layers from the lemongrass stalks. Chop the stalks finely and put the lemongrass in a medium bowl. Add the tamari, garlic, chiles, turmeric, and optional palm sugar and stir until well combined.

Put a clean, folded dish towel on a work surface and set the tofu slices on top. Cover with another folded towel and put a cutting board on top. Put a 1-pound weight on the board and leave for 20 minutes to expel liquid from the tofu. Remove the weight, cutting board, and towel. Stack the tofu slices and cut into 1-inch cubes. Add the tofu to the lemongrass mixture. Toss carefully to coat all the cubes evenly and set aside to marinate for 1 hour.

Put the oil in a medium skillet over high heat and tilt the skillet back and forth until the oil melts and is evenly distributed. As soon as the oil has released its fragrance, add the tofu, along with the marinade, and use a spatula to gently toss the tofu, ensuring that it cooks evenly. Cook for 2 minutes. Add the peanuts and about half the basil, using the spatula to gently distribute the peanuts and basil. Remove from the heat.

Immediately divide the tofu among four bowls. Top with the remaining basil and serve at once.

Per serving: 245 calories, 16 g protein, 19 g fat (9 g sat), 5 g carbohydrates, 365 sodium, 116 mg calcium, 1 g fiber

FORAGING FOR FLAVOR

As its name indicates, lemongrass is a reed-like plant. With a distinct flavor reminiscent of lemon, lemongrass is used throughout southeast Asia, adding its unmistakable signature to the cuisines of Burma, Cambodia, Laos, Thailand, Vietnam, Malaysia, and Indonesia.

OPTIONAL CHEAT: The optional palm sugar coaxes flavor out of chiles and brightens the overall effect of this dish. It's listed as optional because the dish will be fine without it, but why settle for fine when a mere teaspoon of palm sugar will take the dish to superlative? Your call.

t's time for a little modern-day foraging. If you have an Asian market near you, make a trip and see if you can find both oyster mushrooms and the very small Szechuan-style baby bok choy, which are sold in clusters about the size of an apple. While you're there, you'll also want to look for a panang curry paste that does not contain shrimp.

oyster mushroom and baby bok choy CURRY

See photo facing page 74.

MAKES 4 SERVINGS

12 ounces **firm tofu,** cut into ½-inch cubes (optional)

1 tablespoon low-sodium **tamari** (optional)

1 pound **oyster mushrooms**

8 ounces **baby bok choy**

2 tablespoons **extra-virgin coconut oil**

2 tablespoons **panang or red curry paste**

1 can (15 ounces) full-fat **coconut milk**

½ cup coarsely chopped **fresh cilantro**

4 **scallions,** thinly sliced on a sharp diagonal, for garnish

Put the optional tofu and optional tamari in a medium bowl and toss gently. Set aside.

Quarter the mushrooms lengthwise. If the bok choy clusters are very small, they may be left whole or quartered lengthwise; otherwise, cut them crosswise into slices about ½-inch wide.

Put a large saucepan over high heat and add the oil. Tilt the saucepan back and forth until the oil melts and is evenly distributed. Add the mushrooms and bok choy. Stir briskly to prevent sticking until the bok choy wilts, about 1 minute. Stir in the curry paste until well distributed. Add the coconut milk and stir until well combined. Bring to a boil, decrease the heat to medium, and simmer until the mushrooms are tender, about 4 minutes. Add the tofu, if using, and warm through, about 5 minutes. Remove from the heat and stir in the cilantro.

Divide among four bowls and garnish generously with the scallions. Serve at once.

Per serving: 241 calories, 6 g protein, 18 g fat (16 g sat), 14 g carbohydrates, 428 mg sodium, 217 mg calcium, 4 g fiber

J ust as tofu is not traditionally paleo, this is by no means a traditional Thai curry. However, it's rich and satisfying enough to appease your primal cravings. Be sure the basil is firmly packed as directed so you get the maximum flavor possible.

onion and green pepper CURRY

MAKES 4 SERVINGS

1 pound **firm tofu,** cut into ½-inch cubes

1 tablespoon low-sodium **tamari**

2 tablespoons **extra-virgin coconut oil**

2 large **onions,** cut into ¾-inch dice

2 large **green bell peppers,** cut into ¾-inch dice

¼ teaspoon **sea salt**

3 tablespoons **green or red curry paste**

1 can (15 ounces) full-fat **coconut milk**

1 cup fresh **basil leaves,** firmly packed

Toss the tofu gently with the tamari in a medium bowl and set aside.

Put the oil in a large saucepan over high heat. Tilt the saucepan back and forth until the oil melts and is evenly distributed. Add the onions and cook, stirring briskly and frequently, until the onions begin to brown lightly, about 8 minutes. Add the bell peppers and salt and stir until well combined. Cook, stirring frequently, until the bell peppers begin to blister and brown lightly, about 5 minutes. Add the curry paste and cook, stirring until the paste is well distributed. Add the coconut milk and stir until well combined. Bring to a boil, decrease the heat to medium, and simmer for 4 minutes. Add the tofu and warm through, about 5 minutes. Remove from the heat. Chop the basil very coarsely and stir into the curry.

Divide among four bowls. Serve at once.

Per serving: 455 calories, 19 g protein, 34 g fat (23 g sat), 19 g carbohydrates, 609 mg sodium, 148 mg calcium, 3 g fiber

The sauce in this recipe is very rich and tasty but not very spicy, so you may want to add some heat to the food as you sit around the fire. Pass a bowl of diced chiles or a bottle of sriracha sauce separately for those who enjoy a fiery experience.

massaman curry WITH GAI LAN AND PEANUTS

MAKES 4 SERVINGS

1 tablespoon **extra-virgin coconut oil**

12 **scallions,** sliced

3 tablespoons **massaman or red curry paste**

1 tablespoon seedless **tamarind paste** or freshly squeezed **lime juice**

1 can (15 ounces) full-fat **coconut milk**

1½ pounds **gai lan,** cut crosswise at 1-inch intervals (see Foraging for Flavor)

1 cup raw **peanuts**

Put a large saucepan over high heat and add the oil. Tilt the saucepan back and forth until the oil melts and is evenly distributed. Add the scallions and stir briskly for 1 minute. Add the curry paste and tamarind paste and stir until well distributed. Add the coconut milk and gai lan and stir until well combined. Bring to a boil, decrease the heat to medium, add the peanuts, and simmer for about 4 minutes.

Divide among four bowls. Serve at once.

Per serving: 507 calories, 14 g protein, 42 g fat (21 g sat), 24 g carbohydrates, 441 mg sodium, 250 mg calcium, 9 g fiber

FORAGING FOR FLAVOR

Also called Chinese broccoli, gai lan is an Asian vegetable. It's quite similar to broccoli, except the flowering tops are smaller, the stems are thinner, and the leaves are larger. These three parts of the plant are eaten.

CHAPTER NINE

the heart of the hearth . . .

vegetables

For our paleo ancestors and savvy folks from all ages, vegetables have been the heart of the hearth and the center of the diet. Representative of that tradition, this quick-and-easy dish has an interesting character, in part because of the roasted peppers' robust flavor. Be careful not to overcook the kale, so it remains bright green.

kale WITH PEPPERS
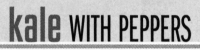

See photo facing page 59.

MAKES 4 SERVINGS

1 large bunch **kale** (about 8 stalks)

2 tablespoons **extra-virgin olive oil**

2 cloves **garlic,** minced or pressed

½ teaspoon **red chile flakes**

¼ teaspoon **sea salt**

2 **red bell peppers,** roasted (see sidebar, page 41), and sliced about ½-inch thick

Freshly ground **black pepper**

Tear the kale into small pieces, discarding the tough center ribs. Fill a large pot about two-thirds full with salted water and bring to a boil over high heat. Drop in the kale, pushing it under the water with a spoon. Cook until the kale is just tender, about 3 minutes, and drain in a colander. Press down with the back of the spoon to squeeze out as much of the water as possible.

Put the oil, garlic, chile flakes, and salt in a medium skillet over medium-low heat. As soon as the garlic and chile flakes begin to sizzle, stir briskly to prevent sticking. Add the roasted bell peppers and stir until well coated. Cook, stirring occasionally, for 2 minutes. Add the kale and stir until well combined. Increase the heat to high and cook, stirring constantly, until the kale is warmed through. Season with pepper to taste. Serve at once.

Per serving: 177 calories, 7 g protein, 8 g fat (1 g sat), 23 g carbohydrates, 228 mg sodium, 280 mg calcium, 5 g fiber

Purple sweet potatoes are a fairly new phenomenon in most places. They're quite similar in taste to the familiar orange variety, but their color is striking. Cooked on the stove top as opposed to baked, sweet potatoes have a firmer texture and work well with the other ingredients in the dish. If you can't find the purple variety, the orange kind will taste just as good.

purple sweet potatoes WITH SCALLIONS AND GINGER

MAKES 4 SERVINGS

2 tablespoons **extra-virgin coconut oil**

1½ cups diced **red onions**

4 fresh **red or green chiles,** finely diced

4 cloves **garlic,** minced or pressed

3 cups sliced **scallions**

2 tablespoons peeled and grated fresh **ginger**

3 cups diced **purple sweet potatoes, garnet yams, or other sweet potatoes**

¼ teaspoon **sea salt**

1⅓ cups full-fat **coconut milk**

2 tablespoons freshly squeezed **lime juice**

Put the oil in a large saucepan over medium-high heat and add the onions. Cook, stirring frequently, for 2 minutes. Add the chiles and garlic and cook, stirring frequently, for 1 minute. Add the scallions and ginger and cook, stirring frequently, for 2 minutes. Add the sweet potatoes and salt and cook, stirring occasionally, until the mixture is nearly dry, about 4 minutes. Add the coconut milk and stir until well combined. Bring to a boil. Decrease the heat to medium, cover, and simmer, stirring frequently, until the sweet potatoes are tender, about 7 minutes. Remove from the heat and stir in the lime juice. Serve at once.

Per serving: 373 calories, 6 g protein, 19 g fat (19 g sat), 42 g carbohydrates, 183 mg sodium, 225 mg calcium, 7 g fiber

D on't be deceived by the simplicity of this recipe. There is no artichoke dish that more profoundly and richly presents the essence of the artichoke than this one. Once the initial prep is done, the dish is amazingly easy to execute. You may never boil or steam an artichoke again.

ROASTED artichokes

1 **lemon,** halved

4 large **artichokes**

2 tablespoons **extra-virgin olive oil**

¼ teaspoon **sea salt**

¼ teaspoon freshly ground **black pepper**

2 teaspoons chopped fresh **parsley,**
for garnish

See how to prepare an artichoke.
youtu.be/bTvhOyDFVmQ

Preheat the oven to 375 degrees F.

Juice the lemon through a strainer into a medium bowl. Reserve the lemon rinds.

Grasp an artichoke by the stem and snap off the outer leaves until the pale, tender inner leaves are exposed. Cut away the tough, darker-green exterior of the artichoke, exposing the pale inner flesh all the way down the stem. Rub all the exposed areas with the juicy side of the lemon rinds, to prevent discoloration. Quarter the artichokes lengthwise and pare away the hairy choke flush with the flesh. Put the artichoke pieces in the bowl and toss with the lemon juice. Repeat with the remaining three artichokes. Add the oil, salt, and pepper and toss until the artichoke pieces are well coated.

Select a baking dish that will accommodate all the artichoke pieces snugly in one layer. Put the artichokes in the dish, along with the lemon juice mixture. Put the baking dish in the center of the oven and roast the artichokes for 20 minutes. Turn the artichokes and roast for 20 minutes longer, or until tender and nicely browned.

Transfer the artichokes to a serving dish and drizzle any accumulated juices over them. Garnish with the parsley and serve at once, or at room temperature.

Per serving: 157 calories, 4 g protein, 7 g fat (1 g sat), 22 g carbohydrates, 256 mg sodium, 61 mg calcium, 11 g fiber

This is both simple enough to be a regular dinner item and elegant enough to offer guests. The flavors are complex, yet the preparation is quite easy.

STUFFED acorn squash

MAKES 4 SERVINGS

2 **Table Queen or other acorn squashes**

4 tablespoons unsalted **vegetable broth**

½ teaspoon **sea salt**

¼ teaspoon freshly ground **black pepper**

2 tablespoons **extra-virgin olive oil**

⅔ cup diced **onion**

½ cup diced **leek,** white part only (see sidebar, page 47)

1½ cups diced **red cabbage**

3 cups diced **romaine lettuce**

1 tart **apple,** diced

½ teaspoon **baharat** (see Foraging for Flavor) **or ground allspice**

1 cup whole **pecans**

2 tablespoons **currants**

2 tablespoons chopped fresh **parsley** (optional)

Zest of 1 **lemon**

Preheat the oven to 375 degrees F.

Cut the squashes in half lengthwise and scoop out the seeds. Discard the seeds. Arrange the squashes in a baking pan, cut-side up. Put 1 tablespoon of the broth in the cavity of each squash half and sprinkle with half the salt and half the pepper. Cover the pan. If the pan has no appropriate lid, cover the squashes with a sheet of parchment paper to keep them moist. Bake for about 1 hour, or until tender. Decrease the oven temperature to 300 degrees F.

Put the oil in a large saucepan over medium-high heat and add the onion and leek. Cook, stirring frequently, for 2 minutes. Add the cabbage and cook, stirring frequently, for 4 minutes. Add the lettuce and cook, stirring frequently, for 3 minutes. Add the apple, baharat, and the remaining salt and pepper and stir until well combined. Cook, stirring frequently, until the vegetables are tender, about 10 minutes. Remove from the heat and stir in the pecans, currants, 1 tablespoon of the optional parsley, and the lemon zest.

Divide the mixture among the four squashes, forming mounds in the cavity of each squash half. Press gently to compact the mounds. Put the squashes in the oven until reheated, about 15 minutes. Garnish with the remaining parsley and serve at once.

Per serving: 421 calories, 6 g protein, 27 g fat (3 g sat), 47 g carbohydrates, 304 mg sodium, 167 mg calcium, 15 g fiber

FORAGING FOR FLAVOR

Baharat is a ground spice mixture used in the cuisines of Iraq and the Gulf states of the Arabian peninsula. It contains black pepper, cardamom seeds, cinnamon, cloves, coriander seeds, cumin seeds, nutmeg, and paprika. Baharat adds a layer of bright, exotic flavor to anything it touches. It can be found at specialty stores and online spice sources.

Squashes, tomato, and basil are a heavenly combination, and the addition of a stellar sauce made rich with cashew cream puts this dish way over the top. Serve this on its own, in a shallow soup bowl, for dramatic effect.

pattypan squash WITH CREAMY TOMATO-BASIL SAUCE

MAKES 4 SERVINGS

½ cup raw **cashews**

¼ cup **water,** plus more as needed

1 tablespoons **extra-virgin olive**

1¼ pounds **baby pattypan squashes,** cut into bite-sized wedges

½ teaspoon **sea salt**

⅛ teaspoon freshly ground **black pepper**

1 cup unsalted **tomato purée**

1 cup coarsely chopped fresh **basil**

To make the cashew cream, put the cashews in a small bowl and cover with boiling water by at least 1 inch. Let soak for 1 hour. Drain and rinse the cashews and put them in a blender with the ¼ cup of water. Process until smooth, adding additional water, 1 tablespoon at a time, as needed to keep the mixture moving. Scrape the cashew cream into a small bowl and set aside.

Put the oil in a medium saucepan over medium-high heat and add the squashes. Stir briskly until the squashes are coated with the oil, about 1 minute. Add the salt and pepper and stir until well combined. Cover and cook, stirring frequently, until the squashes are just tender and beginning to brown, about 10 minutes. Add the tomato purée and stir until well combined. Add the cashew cream and stir until well combined. If the mixture is very thick, add 1 to 2 tablespoons of water until the desired consistency is achieved. Cook, stirring frequently, until the mixture is hot and bubbling. Add the basil and stir until well combined. Remove from the heat and serve at once.

Per serving: 123 calories, 3 g protein, 7 g fat (1 g sat), 14 g carbohydrates, 300 mg sodium, 26 mg calcium, 5 g fiber

Because they're wild and not cultivated, fiddleheads are strictly a foraged food, available only in spring. When you can get very fresh ones, they're well worth the wait. This dish is quite simple and showcases the fiddleheads' delicacy.

SAUTÉED fiddlehead ferns

MAKES 4 SERVINGS

5 cups **fiddlehead ferns**

2 tablespoons **extra-virgin olive oil**

2 **shallots,** finely diced

¼ teaspoon **sea salt**

Freshly ground **black pepper**

Wash the fiddleheads well and trim off any oxidized ends. Put the fiddleheads in a steamer and steam until they are tender-crisp, about 4 minutes. Refresh under cold running water and drain well.

Put the oil in a large saucepan over medium-high heat. Add the shallots and stir briskly. Decrease the heat to medium-low and cook, stirring frequently, until the shallots are just beginning to color lightly, about 10 minutes. Add the salt and a grind or two of pepper. Stir in the fiddleheads and warm through. Serve at once.

Per serving: 124 calories, 7 g protein, 8 g fat (1 g sat), 12 g carbohydrates, 143 mg sodium, 7 mg calcium, 2 g fiber

Portobello mushrooms are by far the best vegetarian choice for grilling. They cook beautifully, with firm flesh and an unparalleled smoky flavor. In this dish, they're paired with a slightly spicy, smoky sauce that is made creamy by cashews and brings out this mushroom's wild side.

grilled portobello mushrooms WITH SMOKY LIME CREAM

MAKES 4 SERVINGS

1 cup raw **cashews**

3 tablespoons freshly squeezed **lime juice**

1½ teaspoons crushed **Aleppo pepper,** or ½ teaspoon **cayenne**

½ teaspoon **Spanish smoked paprika**

½ teaspoon **sea salt**

¼ cup **extra-virgin olive oil**

1 tablespoon chopped fresh **oregano**

4 **portobello mushrooms,** stems removed

¼ teaspoon freshly ground **black pepper**

To make the smoky lime cream, put the cashews in a medium bowl and cover with boiling water by at least 1 inch. Let soak for 1 hour. Drain and rinse the cashews.

Put the cashews in a blender. Add the lime juice, Aleppo pepper, paprika, and ¼ teaspoon of the salt. Process until smooth, adding a little water, 1 teaspoon at a time, as needed to obtain a creamy sauce that's thin enough to drizzle. Pour into a small pitcher or squeeze bottle and set aside.

Preheat the oven to 300 degrees F.

Preheat a grill until very hot. Put the oil and the oregano in a small bowl and stir until well combined. Brush the oil mixture over both sides of the mushrooms. Season with the remaining ¼ teaspoon of salt and the pepper and put on the grill, stem-side down. Cover the grill and cook the mushrooms for 2 minutes. Turn the mushrooms and cook until pools of juice gather in the mushroom caps, 2 to 3 minutes. Remove the mushrooms carefully to avoid spilling the accumulated juices, invert into an oven-proof dish, and cover tightly. Put in the oven to keep warm until ready to serve.

Cut each mushroom into ½-inch slices, keeping the slices together in the original mushroom shape. Using a spatula, lift the mushrooms onto four plates, fanning the slices slightly. Spoon any accumulated juice over the mushrooms, then drizzle the smoky lime cream sauce back and forth over the slices in a decorative pattern. Serve at once.

Per serving: 242 calories, 6 g protein, 20 g fat (3 g sat), 12 g carbohydrates, 285 mg sodium, 12 mg calcium, 3 g fiber

Hazelnut-Chocolate Bark, *page 122*

Butternut Squash with Hazelnuts, page 107

The mere addition of roasted hazelnuts and a little spice takes butternut squash from humdrum to extraordinary. The nuts provide an unexpected crunch that is so alluring, you won't want to stop eating. And the Aleppo pepper intertwines with the allspice to deliver a mysterious, barely perceptible Middle Eastern undertone.

butternut squash WITH HAZELNUTS

See photo facing page.

MAKES 4 SERVINGS

1 medium **butternut squash**
(about 3½ pounds)

1 teaspoon **extra-virgin coconut oil**

¼ cup **flax oil**

½ teaspoon ground **allspice**

¼ teaspoon **sea salt**

¼ teaspoon freshly ground **black pepper**

¼ teaspoon crushed **Aleppo pepper**
(optional; see Foraging for Flavor)

1 cup **hazelnuts**, roasted, peeled, and
coarsely chopped (see sidebar,
page 61)

1 tablespoon snipped fresh **chives**,
for garnish

Preheat the oven to 400 degrees F.

Cut the squash in half lengthwise. Rub a sheet of parchment paper with the coconut oil and put the parchment on a baking sheet, oil-side up. Put the squash on the parchment, cut-side down. Bake for 45 minutes. Decrease the oven temperature to 325 degrees F and continue baking for 30 minutes. Scoop out the seeds with a spoon and discard. Scoop the flesh into a large bowl and mash with a potato masher or silicone spatula. Add the flax oil, allspice, salt, pepper, and optional Aleppo pepper and stir until well combined. Reserve ¼ cup of the hazelnuts and stir the remaining ¾ cup of hazelnuts into the squash until well distributed.

Divide the squash among four bowls. Sprinkle with the reserved hazelnuts and garnish with the chives. Serve at once.

Per serving: 500 calories, 8 g protein, 36 g fat (4 g sat), 47 g carbohydrates, 155 mg sodium, 206 mg calcium, 10 g fiber

FORAGING FOR FLAVOR

Aleppo pepper imparts a very complex note to this dish. If the more exotic Aleppo pepper isn't available, cayenne would certainly suffice to add heat.

Did you know that fennel bulbs come in both male and female forms? The males are flatter and their flesh is thinner, whereas the females are rounder and fleshier. Choose female fennel bulbs for this dish, if possible. Fennel purée goes very well with wild mushrooms and anything grilled or roasted, and that sounds like a classic paleo combo to me.

fennel PURÉE

MAKES 4 SERVINGS

4 large **fennel bulbs**, with fronds

½ cup **flax oil**

2 cups **water**

2 tablespoons **absinthe or Pernod** (optional; see Foraging for Flavor)

1 tablespoon freshly squeezed **lemon juice**

¼ teaspoon **salt**

Freshly ground **black pepper**

1 tablespoon lightly chopped **fennel fronds**, for garnish

Fill a small pot about two-thirds full with water and bring to a boil over high heat. Meanwhile, remove the fronds from the fennel stems and rinse in a colander. Coarsely chop the fronds until you have about 1 tablespoon of chopped fronds and set aside. Put the remaining fronds in the boiling water. Stir once, drain in the colander, and refresh under cold running water. Wrap the fronds in a paper towel and squeeze out as much water as possible. Put the fronds in a blender and add the flax oil. Process on high speed until the oil turns bright green, about 2 minutes. Strain the oil into a small pitcher.

Cut off the fennel stems and save for another use or discard. Trim the fennel bulbs to remove any discolored areas, then chop them coarsely. Put the fennel in a large saucepan and add the water, optional absinthe, lemon juice, and salt. Bring to a boil. Decrease the heat to medium, cover, and simmer until the water has been absorbed and the fennel is very soft, about 25 minutes. Do not let the water evaporate completely or the fennel will stick and burn. If you need to add water, add 1 tablespoon at a time, checking often. Remove from the heat and transfer the fennel to a food processor. Process until smooth. Transfer the purée to the saucepan and reheat over medium heat until hot, 3 to 5 minutes, before serving. If the purée seems a little too runny, cook, stirring constantly, to remove excess moisture and thicken, about 5 minutes.

Divide the purée among four plates, forming mounds. Flatten the tops of the mounds and drizzle 1 tablespoon of the fennel-infused flax oil over each of the mounds. Use a skewer or knife tip to swirl the oil in a decorative pattern. Garnish with the reserved chopped fronds and serve at once.

Per serving: 333 calories, 3 g protein, 28 g fat (3 g sat), 20 g carbohydrates, 262 mg sodium, 115 mg calcium, 7 g fiber

FORAGING FOR FLAVOR

Absinthe is distilled from anise, fennel, and other herbs and will add fennel flavor. At the same time, it will bring the mildly bitter taste of wormwood, a digestive herb, to the mix. Pernod is a liqueur made from fennel, and here it will boost the fennel flavor. Of the two, absinthe is preferable, but Pernod will certainly do an adequate job.

Burdock root is not well known, and this might be because of its odd appearance—it looks something like a long, slightly withered carrot coated with black dirt. But scrubbed and sautéed until tender, burdock root is unequaled in flavor. In this dish, burdock root and Jerusalem artichokes (see Foraging for Flavor, page 51) are slowly roasted and then puréed together to yield an unparalleled woodsy effect, at once coarse and smooth.

burdock root and jerusalem artichoke PURÉE

MAKES 4 SERVINGS

1½ pounds **burdock root**, scrubbed, peeled, and thinly sliced

1 pound **Jerusalem artichokes**, peeled and sliced

½ cup unsalted **vegetable broth**

2 tablespoons low-sodium **tamari**

7 cloves **garlic**, sliced

¼ teaspoon **sea salt**

¼ teaspoon freshly ground **black pepper**

¼ cup **flax oil** (optional)

1 tablespoon chopped fresh **parsley**, for garnish

Preheat the oven to 375 degrees F.

Put the burdock root, Jerusalem artichokes, broth, tamari, garlic, salt, and pepper in a baking dish and toss until well combined. Cut a piece of parchment paper about 1 inch larger than the circumference of the dish and put it on top of the vegetables, pressing down to make contact. (The parchment paper will help discourage evaporation and keep the vegetables moist.) Cover tightly with a lid or foil and put in the oven. Roast for about 1½ hours, or until the vegetables are very tender (the burdock root will remain a little fibrous). Check every 20 minutes to make sure enough broth remains to prevent the vegetables from burning. If necessary, add water, a few tablespoons at a time, and check frequently toward the end of the cooking time.

Transfer the vegetables to a food processor and process until smooth. For a very smooth purée, push the purée through a fine-mesh strainer with a firm silicone spatula. Transfer the purée to a medium saucepan and reheat over medium heat until hot, 3 to 5 minutes. If the purée seems a little too runny, increase the heat to medium-high and cook until thickened, stirring constantly to prevent scorching. Remove from the heat and stir in the optional oil. Serve at once, garnished with the parsley.

Per serving: 219 calories, 6 g protein, 0 g fat (0 g sat), 51 g carbohydrates, 595 mg sodium, 102 mg calcium, 7 g fiber

Foraging for wild mushrooms is fun. Cleaning them, however, definitely feels like work. A lot of care must be taken to remove every trace of grit that might ruin the pleasure of eating them. And, of course, this step must be done without damaging the mushrooms' tender flesh. But once the cleaning is done, the rest is a breeze. And what a delight awaits! Nothing compares to the flavor of sautéed fresh wild mushrooms.

wild mushroom SAUTÉ

MAKES 4 SERVINGS

2 pounds mixed **wild mushrooms, such as morel, porcini, chanterelle, shiitake, or maitake**

3 tablespoons **extra-virgin olive oil**

½ teaspoon **sea salt**

½ teaspoon freshly ground **black pepper**

1 cup thinly sliced **scallions**

1 tablespoon freshly squeezed **lemon juice**

Wash the mushrooms thoroughly and carefully to remove every last bit of dirt and avoid bruising or tearing them. Lay the mushrooms on a clean dish towel to dry before proceeding.

Put the oil in a large saucepan over high heat and add the mushrooms. Toss the mushrooms to coat them with the oil. Cover and cook until the mushrooms begin to release their juices, 1 to 2 minutes. Remove the cover and stir in the salt and pepper. Cook, stirring often, until the juices are absorbed and the mushrooms begin to brown, about 5 minutes. Add the scallions and stir just until they wilt. Remove from the heat and stir in the lemon juice until well combined. Serve at once.

Per serving: 188 calories, 5 g protein, 10 g fat (1 g sat), 24 g carbohydrates, 285 mg sodium, 18 mg calcium, 5 g fiber

Tuscan kale is perfect in this dish. Its tender leaves become silky smooth and succulent when combined with the olive oil and olives.

tuscan kale WITH CHILI, GARLIC, AND BLACK OLIVES

MAKES 4 SERVINGS

1 pound **Tuscan kale leaves,** center ribs removed

4 tablespoons **extra-virgin olive oil,** plus more as needed for drizzling

2 cloves **garlic,** thinly sliced

½ teaspoon **red chile flakes,** plus more as needed

½ cup whole, unpitted black **Niçoise or Ligurian olives** (see Foraging for Flavor)

Sea salt

Freshly ground **black pepper**

Tear the kale leaves into pieces no longer than 4 inches each. Fill a large pot about two-thirds full with salted water and bring to a boil over high heat. Drop in the kale, pushing it under the water with a spoon. Cook until the kale is just tender, about 3 minutes, and drain in a colander. Press down with the back of the spoon to squeeze out as much of the water as possible.

Put the oil, garlic, and chile flakes in a medium skillet over medium heat. When the garlic and chile flakes begin to sizzle, add the olives and cook, stirring briskly to prevent sticking. As soon as the garlic begins to color lightly, add the kale and stir until coated. Increase the heat to high and cook, stirring constantly, until hot, 3 to 5 minutes. Remove from the heat. Season with salt and pepper to taste.

Divide among four plates and serve at once. If you like, pass a small pitcher of olive oil for drizzling.

Per serving: 203 calories, 4 g protein, 14 g fat (2 g sat), 11 g carbohydrates, 47 mg sodium, 18 mg calcium, 2 g fiber

FORAGING FOR FLAVOR

If you can't find Niçoise or Ligurian olives, try kalamatas; they're larger, but they have excellent color and flavor. Whole, unpitted olives are called for in this dish. In the Stone Age, of course, people would have just spat the pits into the fire, but in our time it might be a civilized gesture to provide a small dish for each diner to deposit the pits as they eat.

You may have been advised to "eat the rainbow," meaning that you should eat colorful whole foods because they provide a range of essential nutrients and valuable phytochemicals. I'd add that you should also experience all the tastes—sweet, sour, salty, umami (which roughly translates as "savory"), and the one that many people avoid, bitter. This tantalizing dish offers an opportunity to enjoy this special taste, along with abundant health benefits.

bitter melon CURRY

MAKES 4 SERVINGS

4 **Indian bitter melons,** or 2 **Chinese bitter melons** (see Foraging for Flavor, page 36)

1 (2-inch) piece fresh **ginger,** peeled

2 tablespoons **extra-virgin coconut oil**

2 tablespoons **Thai red curry paste**

4 small **Roma tomatoes,** cut into 1- to 2-inch pieces

1 can (15 ounces) full-fat **coconut milk**

Sea salt

½ cup coarsely chopped fresh **basil leaves**

Cut the bitter melons in half lengthwise and scoop out and discard the seeds. Cut the melons at a sharp angle into slices about ½-inch thick. Cut the ginger into ¼-inch rounds. Lay the ginger rounds on a cutting board and mash them lightly by placing the flat side of a knife on them and striking the knife with the palm of your hand.

Put the oil in a large saucepan over high heat. As soon as the oil melts, add the bitter melon and ginger and cook for 1 minute, stirring constantly to prevent sticking or burning. Add the curry paste and stir to distribute the paste evenly. Stir in the tomatoes and coconut milk and bring to a boil. Decrease the heat, cover, and simmer until the vegetables are tender and the tomatoes have disintegrated into the sauce, about 25 minutes. Season with salt to taste. Remove from the heat and stir in the basil. Serve at once.

Per serving: 284 calories, 3 protein, 25 g fat (22 g sat), 13 g carbohydrates, 194 mg sodium, 12 mg calcium, 3 g fiber

This dish derives most of its flavor from a sea vegetable, so you wouldn't expect it to have such a distinctly earthy quality. Eating it produces a warm, grounding effect. The secret to making this richly satisfying but unpretentious dish is to take your time, completing each step before moving on to the next one.

carrots, hijiki, and onions

MAKES 4 SERVINGS

½ cup dried **hijiki**

1 tablespoon **extra-virgin coconut oil or extra-virgin olive oil**

2 medium **onions,** halved and cut lengthwise into slivers about ¼-inch wide

4 cups grated **carrots**

3 tablespoons low-sodium **tamari,** plus more as needed

2 tablespoons **mirin**

2 tablespoons **sake** (optional)

1 teaspoon **toasted sesame oil**

Rinse the hijiki and put it in a medium bowl. Cover with water by 1 inch. Let stand for at 20 minutes to reconstitute. Drain, reserving the soaking liquid.

Put the coconut oil in a large saucepan over medium-high heat and add the onions. Cook, stirring frequently, until the onions begin to brown, about 10 minutes. Add the carrots and hijiki and stir until well combined. Cook, stirring frequently, until the mixture is nearly dry and beginning to stick, about 15 minutes. Add the tamari and cook, stirring frequently, until nearly dry. Add the mirin, optional sake, and the hijiki soaking liquid and stir until well combined. Cook, stirring occasionally, until the liquid is absorbed, about 10 minutes. Remove from the heat and stir in the toasted sesame oil. Serve at once.

Per serving: 161 calories, 3 g protein, 5 g fat (3 g sat), 25 g carbohydrates, 704 mg sodium, 160 mg calcium, 6 g fiber

FORAGING FOR FLAVOR

- One of many sea vegetables used in Japan, hijiki, or hiziki, is sold in dried form and looks like a tangle of hard, black strings. After it's been reconstituted in water, hijiki resembles small twigs. Its flavor is strong and briny. Hijiki can be found in natural food stores, among the macrobiotic foods.

- Mirin is a sweet sake, or rice wine, used as a seasoning in Japanese cuisine.

This dish combines green beans with *piperade*, a spicy sauce common in Basque cooking. The sauce calls for piment d'Espelette, a red chile that grows in the Basque region, on the French side of the Pyrenees Mountains. If you can't find this chile where you live, I suggest using Aleppo pepper, which is more widely available and will bring a special, if quite different, flavor to the dish.

BASQUE-STYLE green beans

MAKES 4 SERVINGS

1 pound very fresh **green beans,** stemmed and cut in half crosswise

2 tablespoons **extra-virgin olive oil**

1 large **onion,** cut lengthwise into ½-inch strips

1 **green bell pepper,** cut lengthwise into ½-inch strips

1 **red bell pepper,** cut lengthwise into ½-inch strips

3 cloves **garlic,** minced

½ teaspoon **hot paprika**

½ teaspoon ground **piment d'Espelette or crushed Aleppo pepper,** or ¼ teaspoon **cayenne**

½ teaspoon **sea salt**

¼ teaspoon freshly ground **black pepper**

1½ cups peeled, seeded, and diced **Roma tomatoes**

Fill a large pot about two-thirds full with salted water and bring to a boil over high heat. Add the green beans. Cook for 30 seconds, then drain and refresh under cold running water. Drain well.

Put the oil in a large saucepan over medium-high heat and add the onion. Cook, stirring frequently, until the onion is soft and just beginning to brown, about 5 minutes. Stir in the bell peppers. Cook, stirring often, until the bell pepper softens, about 5 minutes. Add the garlic and cook, stirring frequently, for 1 minute. Add the paprika, piment d'Espelette, salt, and pepper and cook, stirring frequently, until well combined, about 1 minute. Add the tomatoes and green beans and stir until well combined. Decrease the heat and cook, stirring frequently, until all the vegetables are tender and the tomatoes have softened into a thick sauce, about 10 minutes. Serve at once.

Per serving: 141 calories, 6 g protein, 8 g fat (1 g sat), 18 g carbohydrates, 300 mg sodium, 61 mg calcium, 7 g fiber

Beets and sweet potatoes met on the hearth long ago—but combining them, as is done in this unique recipe, is a colorful first. Here, both vegetables are purple, lending an intriguing and lovely hue to this dish. In addition, both vegetables are sweet, providing the perfect counterpoint to the miso, a relative newcomer to the beet-and-potato scene.

PURÉE OF roasted beet and purple sweet potato

MAKES 4 SERVINGS

1½ pounds **purple sweet potatoes,** scrubbed

4 cups cubed **beets** (1-inch cubes)

1 tablespoon **extra-virgin olive oil**

¼ teaspoon **sea salt**

¼ teaspoon freshly ground **mixed peppercorns** (black, white, green, and pink) **or black only**

2 tablespoons **mellow white miso**

Preheat the oven to 400 degrees F. Put the sweet potatoes on a baking sheet and bake for 40 minutes.

Turn the oven temperature down to 375 degrees F. Put the beets in a medium bowl and add the oil, salt, and pepper. Toss until well combined. Put the beets in a 1½-quart baking dish and cover with a lid or foil. Bake the beets, along with the sweet potatoes, for 45 minutes.

Remove the sweet potatoes and beets from the oven and let cool. Cut the sweet potatoes in half lengthwise. Scoop out the flesh and put in a food processor. Add the beets and process until smooth. Scrape the mixture into a medium saucepan and reheat, stirring constantly to prevent sticking, until hot, about 5 minutes. Remove from the heat and stir in the miso. Serve at once.

Per serving: 248 calories, 6 g protein, 4 g fat (1 g sat), 49 g carbohydrates, 609 mg sodium, 77 mg calcium, 9 g fiber

Peewee potatoes are about the size of an olive, and they can easily be mistaken for olives in this savory creation, which works as a side dish or an appetizer. Be prepared if you serve it as a first course: guests may stampede to the table, quickly devour your offering, and be primed to start immediately on the next, equally exquisite course.

peewee potatoes WITH OLIVES AND ROSEMARY

MAKES 4 SERVINGS

3 cups **peewee potatoes,** scrubbed (see Foraging for Flavor)

¾ cup **green Sicilian olives, picholines,** or other green olives

¾ cup **pitted kalamata olives,** rinsed and dried

¼ cup **extra-virgin olive oil**

¼ cup chopped fresh **parsley**

Zest of 1 **lemon**

3 tablespoons freshly squeezed **lemon juice**

2 teaspoons chopped fresh **thyme**

1 teaspoon chopped fresh **rosemary**

½ teaspoon **garlic,** pressed

¼ teaspoon freshly ground **black pepper**

Fill a large pot about two-thirds full with salted water and bring to a boil over high heat. Add the potatoes and cook for 10 minutes. Drain and put in a medium bowl.

Cut the flesh from the Sicilian olives and put it in a food processor. Add the kalamata olives, oil, parsley, lemon zest, lemon juice, thyme, rosemary, garlic, and pepper. Pulse until finely chopped but not puréed. Add to the potatoes and toss thoroughly. Serve at once or at room temperature.

Per serving: 211 calories, 2 g protein, 19 g fat (3 g sat), 12 g carbohydrates, 592 mg sodium, 23 mg calcium, 2 g fiber

FORAGING FOR FLAVOR

Peewee potatoes may be difficult to find. If so, substitute with fingerling potatoes or new potatoes, cut into bite-sized pieces.

To prepare this dish successfully, you'll need two things: a distinctive ground chile, such as Chimayó chile, and a grill basket that allows you to grill cut vegetables without them falling through the grate. The beauty of Chimayó chile, which is from New Mexico, is that it packs a potent flavor but not too much heat. Use it confidently to create an intense taste sensation without searing the taste buds.

grilled mixed vegetables WITH GARLIC AND CHILE

MAKES 4 SERVINGS

¾ pound **zucchini**

¾ pound **yellow squashes**

¾ pound **Japanese eggplants**

2 **red bell peppers**

2 **green bell peppers**

1 **yellow bell pepper**

2 large **onions**

⅓ cup **extra-virgin olive oil**

7 cloves **garlic**, minced or pressed

3 tablespoons ground **Chimayó chile** or other distinctive chile

1 teaspoon **sea salt**

1 teaspoon freshly ground **black pepper**

2 tablespoons freshly squeezed **lime juice**

Preheat a grill on high.

Cut the zucchini, yellow squash, eggplant, bell peppers, and onions into bite-sized pieces. Put the oil, garlic, Chimayó chile, salt, and pepper in a large bowl and stir until combined. Add the vegetables and toss thoroughly. Put the vegetables in a grill basket and set on the grill. If the grill has a lid, close it. Cook the vegetables, shaking the basket every few minutes, until they are evenly browned and tender, about 15 minutes. Transfer the vegetables to a serving dish and sprinkle the lime juice over them. Toss briefly and serve at once.

Per serving: 251 calories, 4 g protein, 17 g fat (2 g sat), 21 g carbohydrates, 585 mg sodium, 57 mg calcium, 6 g fiber

ny variety of root vegetables can be prepared this way, but carrots and parsnips share two main attributes—sweetness and basic shape—so they go particularly well together. Once you've done the prep, you can easily make this at the same time as other dishes, but only if you remember to stir the vegetables so they don't burn.

ROASTED carrots and parsnips

2 tablespoons **extra-virgin coconut oil**

4 medium **carrots,** cut into sticks about 2 inches long and ½-inch thick

4 medium **parsnips,** cut into sticks about 2 inches long and ½-inch thick

1 large sprig fresh **rosemary**

½ teaspoon **sea salt**

2 tablespoons chopped fresh **parsley**

⅛ teaspoon freshly ground **black pepper**

Preheat the oven to 400 degrees F.

Put the oil in a medium-large ovenproof skillet over high heat. As soon as the oil melts, add the carrots and parsnips and stir until well combined. Sear the vegetables, turning or tossing them almost constantly, for about 5 minutes. Add the rosemary and salt and stir until well combined. Put the skillet in the oven. Roast the vegetables, stirring frequently, until they are lightly browned and tender, about 30 minutes. Add the parsley and pepper and stir until well combined. Remove the rosemary sprig and serve at once.

Per serving: 159 calories, 3 g protein, 8 g fat (7 g sat), 20 g carbohydrates, 323 mg sodium, 20 mg calcium, 4 g fiber

Grilling asparagus produces a flavor unlike any other cooking method. Sugars you never suspected were there will emerge, with glorious results. In fact, people who don't favor asparagus will likely adore this dish. The addition of roasted bell peppers, lightly caramelized onions, and a touch of smoked paprika creates a stunning, irresistible effect.

grilled asparagus WITH ROASTED PEPPERS AND ONIONS

MAKES 4 SERVINGS

3 tablespoons **extra-virgin olive oil**

1 large **onion**, halved lengthwise and sliced about ¼-inch thick

2 **red bell peppers**, roasted (see sidebar, page 41), and sliced about ¼-inch thick

½ teaspoon **Spanish smoked paprika**

½ teaspoon **sea salt**

½ teaspoon freshly ground **black pepper**

1½ pounds **asparagus**, tough ends removed

½ **lemon**

1 tablespoon chopped fresh **parsley**, for garnish

Put 1½ tablespoons of the oil in a large skillet over high heat and add the onion. Cook, stirring frequently, until the onion is soft and beginning to brown lightly, about 10 minutes. Decrease the heat to medium-high and add the roasted bell peppers. Cook, stirring frequently, for 2 minutes. Stir in the paprika and ¼ teaspoon of the salt. Cook, stirring frequently, for 4 minutes. Stir in ¼ teaspoon of the pepper and decrease the heat to medium-low.

Preheat a grill on high.

Put the asparagus on a baking sheet and brush lightly with the remaining 1½ tablespoons of oil. Season with the remaining salt and pepper. Lay the asparagus spears on the grill, positioning them perpendicular to the grate to prevent them from falling through. Cook for 1 minute, turn, and cook on the other side for 2 minutes. Put the asparagus back on the baking sheet and cover with foil or parchment paper.

When the peppers are warmed through, divide the asparagus among four plates, arranging them in a pile with the tips facing in the same direction. Divide the pepper mixture among the four servings, draping the peppers across the center of the asparagus piles. Squeeze a little lemon juice over each serving and garnish with the parsley. Serve at once.

Per serving: 155 calories, 5 g protein, 10 g fat (1 g sat), 13 g carbohydrates, 287 mg sodium, 54 mg calcium, 5 g fiber

at sundown, healthy delights . . .

desserts

Hazelnut and chocolate are a match made in culinary heaven. The secret to making excellent chocolate is tempering (see sidebar), which involves heating and cooling the chocolate so it acquires a lustrous sheen and snaps when broken. Yet, this dessert is not hard to make, and it will disappear like the dinosaurs: in a paleo minute.

hazelnut-chocolate BARK

See photo facing page 106.

MAKES 1¼ POUNDS, 10 (2-OUNCE) SERVINGS

2 cups **very fresh hazelnuts,** roasted (see Paleo Pointer on the facing page, and sidebar, page 61)

1 pound **dark chocolate,** coarsely chopped

Put about half the hazelnuts on a cutting board and cut them cleanly in half lengthwise. Chop the remaining nuts coarsely. Keep the two separate.

Reserve about 1 ounce of the chocolate and put the rest in a medium bowl. Create a water bath by putting about 2 inches of hot but not boiling water in a shallow bowl. Set the bowl of chocolate in the shallow bowl of water. Stir until the chocolate is completely melted. Move the bowl of chocolate to the countertop and stir in the reserved ounce of chocolate until it has melted. Return the bowl to the water bath and stir for 1 to 2 minutes.

Spread a sheet of heavy-duty aluminum foil (or a silicone baking mat) shiny-side up on the back of a baking sheet. Pour the melted chocolate onto the foil, forming a rough rectangular shape. Smooth the chocolate out with a long metal spatula to an even thickness of about ¼-inch. Set the hazelnut halves cut-side up into the chocolate, pressing the the nuts down lightly. Sprinkle the chopped hazelnuts over the chocolate, covering as much area as possible. Put the baking sheet in the refrigerator until the chocolate has set, about 15 minutes.

Remove from the refrigerator. Pull the chocolate away from the foil and break the chocolate into random pieces about 4 to 5 inches long and 3 to 4 inches wide. Stack the pieces on a plate and dig into them at will. Stored in a tightly sealed container in the refrigerator, the bark will last . . . well, let's face it—it won't last!

Per serving: 177 calories, 4 protein, 16 g fat (4 sat), 14 g carbohydrates, 4 mg sodium, 5 mg calcium, 4 g fiber

If the term "very fresh" is confusing in reference to hazelnuts, the test is quite simple. Just taste them. They should have a little snap to them when you bite down and a very agreeable flavor, with no hint of rancidity. If you like the taste, they're fresh enough for you.

TEMPERING CHOCOLATE: Tempering is a process that involves melting chocolate to a temperature between 115 and 120 degrees F, then letting it cool to 80 degrees or slightly above, then warming it slightly, to between 88 and 91 degrees. If you have a candy thermometer and wish to use it for this recipe, be my guest. If not, just follow the instructions and keep the finished bark in the refrigerator until a few minutes before serving. No worries.

Hot desserts are always perceived as elegant and special. This one is so easy, but you don't have to tell anyone— just let them murmur their approval between bites.

grilled pineapple WITH PINEAPPLE-COCONUT SAUCE

MAKES 4 SERVINGS

1 medium **pineapple**

¼ cup **coconut cream** (see sidebar, page 32)

7 pitted **medjool dates**

1 tablespoon peeled and grated fresh **ginger**

2 teaspoons freshly squeezed **lime juice**

9 **cloves**

2 teaspoons **extra-virgin olive oil**

Preheat a grill on high.

Cut the skin from the pineapple and remove the "eyes." Lay the pineapple on its side on a cutting board and cut four slices about 1 inch thick. Punch out the center of each slice with a 1½-inch biscuit cutter to remove the core and make pineapple rings. Set the pineapple rings aside.

To make the sauce, quarter the remaining pineapple lengthwise and cut away the core. Chop enough of the pineapple to yield 1 cup and put it in a blender. Add the coconut cream, dates, ginger, and lime juice and process until smooth. The sauce should be thick. Pour the sauce into a small bowl. Pinch the round tips off five of the cloves and rub them between your thumb and forefinger to crush them slightly. Add the crushed cloves to the bowl and stir until well combined. Save or discard the clove stems.

Brush both sides of the pineapple rings with the oil and put them on the grill. Press down on the pineapple rings with a spatula to ensure contact with the grill. Cook until grill marks are well defined on the first side, about 2 minutes. Turn over and cook on the other side until grill marks are well defined, about 3 minutes.

Remove the pineapple rings from the grill and put one on each of four dessert plates. Spoon a generous mound of the sauce into the center of each pineapple ring. Pinch a clove tip like before and use your fingers to crush it over one pineapple ring. Repeat with the other three cloves and serve at once.

Per serving: 221 calories, 2 g protein, 5 g fat (3 g sat), 47 g carbohydrates, 5 mg sodium, 4 mg calcium, 5 g fiber

This is an elegant dessert, made all the more classy by the fruits that it showcases so beautifully. It's the perfect finish to a cave-side candlelight dinner. Reducing the port concentrates its flavor and inherent sweetness. Crushing the cardamom seeds just before adding them ensures a bright, spectacular presence overall. And that's really all there is to it.

fuyu persimmons and cherries WITH PORT REDUCTION

MAKES 4 SERVINGS

2 cups fresh **Bing cherries,** or 1 cup dried **unsweetened tart cherries**

2 cups **ruby port**

¼ teaspoon lightly crushed **cardamom seeds**

2 large, firm **fuyu persimmons,** peeled and cut into ¼-inch wedges

1 tablespoon finely julienned **Buddha's-hand or lemon zest** (see Foraging for Flavor and Paleo Pointer), for garnish

Cut the cherries in half and remove the pits. If using dried cherries, put them in a medium saucepan and add the port. Bring to a simmer over medium heat, then remove from the heat and let soak for 30 minutes. Drain the cherries well, saving the port, and set the cherries aside.

Put the port in a medium saucepan over medium-high heat and bring to a boil. Stir in the cardamom seeds. Decrease the heat to medium and cook until the port has reduced to about ½ cup, about 15 minutes. Check frequently to prevent overcooking. Let cool just until warm.

Put the cherries, persimmons, and warm port in a medium bowl and toss gently but thoroughly.

Divide among four dessert bowls. Garnish with the Buddha's-hand and serve at once.

Per serving: 273 calories, 1 g protein, 0 g fat (0 g sat), 27 g carbohydrates, 0 mg sodium, 8 mg calcium, 4 g fiber

FORAGING FOR FLAVOR

Buddha's-hand, a citrus fruit native to Southeast Asia, grows into a distinctive, many-fingered "hand" shape. Unlike most citrus fruits, it is virtually all zest and pith, with no juice, and is used primarily for the unique flavor imparted by the zest, which is most often grated. Buddha's-hand appears in American markets in the early winter to early spring. Choose large, firm, yellow-fleshed fruits with no soft fingers or blemishes.

PALEO POINTER

To julienne the Buddha's-hand, remove strips about 1½ to 2 inches long with a vegetable peeler, then cut lengthwise into thin strips, like matchsticks.

Fresh ginger adds a warming, almost spicy undertone to the filling in this very chocolaty tart. The crust is simply dates and nuts fused together by molten chocolate that becomes firm when it cools but never hardens. And a light dusting of cocoa on top adds just a hint of chocolate's bitter edge to the composition. Chocolate upon chocolate upon chocolate—what's not to love?

ginger-chocolate tart IN A RAW CRUST

MAKES 12 SERVINGS

1 cup **pecans**

1 cup **Brazil nuts**

10 pitted **medjool dates**

¼ cup **cacao nibs** (see Foraging for Flavor)

Pinch **sea salt**

20 ounces **dark chocolate**, chopped

1 tablespoon raw **almond meal** or finely ground **almonds**

1½ cups peeled and chopped fresh **ginger**

2 tablespoons **dark rum** (optional)

1 cup full-fat **coconut milk**

1 tablespoon Dutch-processed **cocoa** (see Foraging for Flavor)

Put the pecans, Brazil nuts, dates, cacao nibs, and salt in a food processor and pulse until chopped into small pieces, ⅛- to ¼-inch in size.

Break off about 4 ounces of chocolate and put it in a medium bowl. Create a water bath by putting about 2 inches of hot but not boiling water in a shallow bowl. Set the bowl of chocolate in the shallow bowl of water. Stir until the chocolate is completely melted. Pour the chocolate over the chopped nuts and dates and pulse until thoroughly mixed.

To make the crust, sprinkle the almond meal evenly over the removable bottom of a 9-inch tart pan. Press the date-nut mixture into the bottom and up the sides of the pan and refrigerate until firm, about 30 minutes. This will be a sticky procedure, but the crust will firm up once refrigerated.

To make the filling, put the remaining 16 ounces of chocolate in a blender and add the ginger and optional rum. Put the coconut milk in a small saucepan over medium-high heat and bring to a simmer. Remove from the heat for 10 seconds, then pour into the blender over the chocolate mixture. Process until smooth. Pour the filling into the crust, straining it if necessary to remove any ginger fibers. Carefully transfer the tart to the refrigerator and let it set up for 3 hours before serving.

Remove the tart from the refrigerator 20 minutes before serving. Dust the top with the cocoa by tapping spoonfuls through a fine-mesh strainer to disperse it. Cut the tart with a hot, dry knife and serve.

Per serving: 309 calories, 6 g protein, 27 g fat (10 g sat), 28 g carbohydrates, 18 mg sodium, 53 mg calcium, 7 g fiber

FORAGING FOR FLAVOR

- Crushed raw cacao beans are called "nibs," and they are an extremely healthful food, with reputedly up to four times the antioxidant content of green tea. They're also a delicious bittersweet, crunchy treat.

- Dutch-processed cocoa, also known as alkalized cocoa, is a double-edged sword. On the one hand, it is much more palatable than raw cacao, with very little bitterness, and it dissolves much more readily in liquids; on the other, the processing unfortunately removes a great deal of cacao's health benefits. Recommended uses are for desserts and hot cocoa drinks, where the loss of antioxidants may be an acceptable trade-off for a smooth, delectable chocolate experience.

Figs and chocolate—two of nature's most glorious accomplishments—join together to offer a sensual treat, made even more luscious by the bright, cool touch of fresh mint. All the steps can be done ahead, except for the cutting of the mint, making this the ideal dessert for entertaining.

figs WITH CHOCOLATE BALSAMIC VINEGAR

MAKES 4 SERVINGS

½ cup **balsamic vinegar**

2 tablespoons raw **cacao** (see Foraging for Flavor)

16 ripe **figs**, stemmed and quartered lengthwise

8 large fresh **mint leaves,** for garnish

Put the vinegar in a small saucepan and bring to a boil over medium-high heat. Simmer until reduced by half, about 15 minutes. Add the cacao and whisk until dissolved. Remove from the heat.

Put the figs in a large bowl and add the vinegar mixture. Toss gently but thoroughly.

Divide among four dessert bowls. Stack the mint leaves and cut crosswise into strips about ⅛-inch wide. Fluff the strips to separate them and sprinkle over the figs. Serve at once.

Per serving: 183 calories, 1 g protein, 1 g fat (0.2 g sat), 48 g carbohydrates, 15 mg sodium, 85 mg calcium, 5 g fiber

FORAGING FOR FLAVOR

Not all raw cacao is palatable without some form of sweetener added. I suggest you try a few raw cacao powders and select one that you like.

glossary

Aleppo pepper. For people who don't tolerate spicy food very well, all chiles tend to taste the same; once the heat begins, their taste buds go somewhat numb. Aleppo pepper, a native of northern Syria, is ideal for these folks, because it has a relatively mild bite combined with a lively flavor, reminiscent of sun-dried tomatoes. I use Aleppo pepper frequently because it allows me to pack chile flavor into a dish without making it too spicy.

Allium vegetables. The allium family of vegetables includes red, white, yellow, pearl, and cipolline onions, as well as shallots, garlic, leeks, scallions, ramps, and chives.

Ancho chile powder. Ancho chile is a ripened (red), dried Mexican poblano chile (the fresh, green form is used for chiles rellenos). The flavor is exotic and quite strong, enough to alter the character of a dish dramatically.

Balsamic vinegar, aged. True balsamic vinegar is not a true vinegar but rather a reduction of white Trebbiano grape juice to which a vinegar "mother" is added. This mixture is aged and decanted to a series of wooden casks for a minimum of twelve years. The longer it ages, the thicker and mellower it becomes. An eighteen-year-old balsamic vinegar has beautiful depth of flavor, mild acidity, and a thick and silky consistency, ideal for most uses. The balsamic vinegar generally sold in stores is a less expensive imitation and is not aged in this way. It is much thinner in consistency, with a sharper flavor. An acceptable substitute for aged balsamic can be made by simmering commercial balsamic vinegar over medium-low heat until it is reduced by about 40 percent. This will give it more body and concentrate the flavor.

Bitter melon. A native of East Asia, bitter melon is an acquired taste for most Westerners. In Chinese medicine, it's called "bitter cucumber" and used as a medicinal herb for treating all sorts of ailments, including diabetes and anemia. It's a powerful blood purifier and blood tonic. The best variety is found at Indian grocery stores, where it's known as *karela*.

Cacao, raw. Ground raw cacao retains most of the healthful properties of the cacao plant, and is preferable in most instances for this reason. Although raw cacao generally lacks the refined flavor of Dutch-processed cocoa, some new producers are now offering a very high-quality raw cacao. Taste is the only test for cooks, so try different brands to determine which one works best for you.

Capers. Capers are small, edible flower buds from the caper bush, native to the Mediterranean, that are picked unripe and preserved either by salting or, most commonly, by pickling in a salt-and-vinegar solution. The best capers for culinary use are called nonpareils, and are very small, with intense flavor.

Cardamom seeds. When possible, buy dried cardamom seeds that are still in the pod because the pod protects the aromatics in the seeds. Even if you can't find them in the pods, dried seeds are always preferable to ground cardamom. Crushing or grinding the seeds immediately before using them in recipes ensures the best flavor. Although in Western cuisines cardamom is associated with sweets, in North Africa, the Middle East, and India it is used for both sweet and savory dishes.

Chia seeds. Native to Mesoamerica, chia seeds are a miraculous superfood, high in essential fats, protein, fiber, and minerals. Their hydrophilic quality enables them to absorb ten times their weight in water, which is useful in making healthful puddings and other desserts. This quality is also valuable to athletes, because chia soaked in water will release both nutrients and water slowly, helping athletes stay hydrated over an extended period.

Chimayó chile. Another ground and dried chile that offers a complex flavor with relatively minor heat is the Chimayó of northern New Mexico. It adds a burst of exotic chile flavor without too much heat and brightens up salad dressings, grilled vegetables, and pretty much anything it touches.

Chipotle chile. Chipotle chiles are jalapeño chiles that have been allowed to ripen to a bright red color before being picked, smoked, and dried, which intensifies their flavor and heat. After they're dried, the chiles can be ground to a powder or reconstituted in water and cooked in a sauce, known as adobo. Chipotles in adobo are the most widely available form of chipotles and are sold in small cans in supermarkets.

Coconut milk. Coconut milk is made by blending the coconut water from the interior of the coconut and the white tender flesh on the inside of the shell. It has a sweet, rich flavor and many uses. In Southeast Asia, it's used to make a creamy sauce in curries as well as sweets. Most commonly, coconut milk is sold in cans, but it can also be found frozen at Asian markets.

Étouffé. In French, *étouffé* means "smothered." In culinary terms, it refers to a dish that has been smothered in a rich sauce.

Fines herbes. A staple of French cuisine, fines herbes (literally "fine herbs") is a blend of chives, chervil, tarragon, parsley, and marjoram.

Harissa. The staple hot sauce of Morocco, harissa is a fiery blend of hot red chiles, garlic, caraway seeds, and olive oil. Some versions may include roasted red bell peppers, coriander seeds, cumin seeds, and dried or chopped fresh mint or cilantro.

Hempseeds. A rich source of protein, essential fats, and fiber, hulled hempseeds are very tender and can be used to make hempseed milk; simply process them in a blender with water. They can also be used in smoothies for added protein, in sauces and dressings to add creaminess, or on salads or vegetables as a crunchy topping.

Hijiki. One of many sea vegetables used in Japan, hijiki (also called hiziki) is sold in dried form and looks like a tangle of hard, black strings. After it's been reconstituted in water, hijiki resembles small twigs. Its flavor is strong and briny. Hijiki can be found in natural food stores, among the macrobiotic foods.

Miso. Miso is a fermented soybean paste that is used primarily in Japanese cuisine. There are different kinds of miso, some quite strong in flavor, but the recipes in this book that call for it refer to mellow white miso, the mildest tasting version.

Picholine olives. A small green olive grown in southern France, the picholine has a profound yet delicate herbaceous flavor, pleasantly firm texture, and smooth finish. It's ideal as a cocktail olive, but it also makes an excellent snack.

Piperade. A staple of the Basque cuisine, in the mountainous region on the border between France and Spain, *piperade* is a spicy sauce made with onions, peppers, tomatoes, and a mildly hot chile pepper native to the region, called *piment d'Espelette*.

Red chile powder. Indian grocery stores carry a very hot and fragrant red chile powder, but cayenne is a passable substitute.

Spanish smoked paprika. Called *pimenton picante* in Spain, this paprika is made from mildly hot pimento peppers that are smoked, dried, and then ground. Once hard to find in America, this spice is now quite widely available. A little goes a long way to add a delicious smoky, piquant flavor to a sauce, a dressing, or any dish.

Tabouli. A Lebanese salad, tabouli (also tabbouleh) is made with chopped parsley, scallions, bulgur, olive oil, and lemon juice. Other ingredients may include cucumber, mint, or tomato.

Tahini. A paste made from lightly roasted sesame seeds, tahini (also tahine) is popular in Middle Eastern dishes.

Tamari. Tamari is the Japanese version of its Chinese cousin, soy sauce. Both tamari and soy sauce are made from fermented soybeans, but little or no wheat is added in the making of tamari, which is thicker and less salty, with a more full-bodied flavor. It is advisable to select the low-sodium version whenever possible.

Thai curry paste. In Thai cuisine, various spice combinations of both fresh and dried ingredients are pounded to a smooth paste and then used to flavor curries and other dishes. Each paste has a unique flavor. The most common are green curry, red curry, yellow curry, panang curry, and massaman curry. Traditional Thai curry pastes usually include ground dried shrimp, but some companies produce pastes without the added shrimp. For vegans in particular, reading the list of ingredients on the label is therefore recommended.

Toasted sesame oil. Made from toasted sesame seeds, this traditional Japanese culinary oil is used in small quantities as a seasoning, not for actual cooking.

Tofu. Made from soybeans, tofu (also called bean curd) is a staple in Asian cuisines and is available in a number of varieties, such as silken, soft, and firm. Because commercial soybeans are a genetically engineered crop, it's important to choose organic tofu.

Walnut oil. Milder than olive oil, walnut oil is the ideal choice when you want a salad dressing with a subtle flavor. It's important to choose unrefined walnut oil for both flavor and health. Store walnut oil in the refrigerator to protect the fragile fats.

index

Book Publishing Co.

books that educate, inspire, and empower

To find your favorite vegetarian and soyfood products online, visit:
healthy-eating.com

Extraordinary Vegan
Alan Roettinger
978-1-57067-296-5 • $19.95

Omega 3 Cuisine
Alan Roettinger
Udo Erasmus, PhD
978-0-920470-81-7 • $19.95

Speed Vegan
Alan Roettinger
978-1-57067-244-6 • $19.95

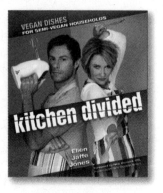

Kitchen Divided
Ellen Jaffe Jones
978-1-57067-292-7 • $19.95

Cooking Vegan
Vesanto Melina, MS, RD
Joseph Forest
978-1-57067-267-5 • $19.95

Eat Vegan on $4 a Day
Ellen Jaffe Jones
978-1-57067-257-6 • $14.95

Purchase these health titles and cookbooks from your local bookstore or natural food store,
or you can buy them directly from:

Book Publishing Company • P.O. Box 99 • Summertown, TN 38483 • 800-695-2241

Please include $3.95 per book for shipping and handling.